The Organic Movement in Michigan

Edited by Maynard Kaufman and Julia Christianson

Published by Michigan Organic Food and Farm Alliance
P.O. Box 26102, Lansing, MI 48909

moffa@moffaorganic.org

ISBN: 978-1542504881

Library of Congress Control Number: 2017907816

CreateSpace Independent Publishing Platform, North Charleston, SC

Cover Design and Illustration by Laura B. DeLind

Dedicated to the writers who have contributed to this book. Not only have they given years of effort to the organic movement—they were willing to write about it.

Contents

Introduction 1

The Early Organic Movement in Michigan 3

PART I: OGM

Organic Growers of Michigan, 1973-2005 7

Chapters of OGM 16
    Southwest 16
    Third Coast 21
    Southeast 23
    Thumb 26
    Lifeline 30

The Organic Certification Program
      After National Organic Standards 34

PART II: MOFFA

Origins of Michigan Organic Food and Farm Alliance 38

MOFFA in the '90s: Enlarging the Organic
      Movement in Michigan 47

MOFFA in the 21st Century 51

PART III: Other Organic Groups and Activities

The Organic Movement at MSU 70

The Student Organic Farm at MSU 81

Organic Farmers of Michigan 93

MDA Organic Advisory Committee 100

Origins of Michigan Land Trustees 105

Community Supported Agriculture in 2002:
   The State of the Art in Michigan 117

Organic Food Co-ops in Michigan: A Case History
   of Oryana Community Co-op 126

BeginningFarmers.org 137

Organic Soil Management 142

**PART IV: Organic Farming, Now More Important
          Than Ever**

Organics—The New Industry 159

The Future of Organic Farming In a Time of
   Global Warming 172

Photo Credits 185

Appendix A: Timeline of the Organic Movement 186

Appendix B   MOFFA Board Members 1992-2017 190

Appendix C: Grants Received by MOFFA 1992-2017 192

Appendix D: Awards Presented by MOFFA 194

Appendix E: Glossary of Acronyms 196

Index 199

Introduction

Maynard Kaufman, Editor

Why bother to publish a book on the organic movement in Michigan? Plans are being made for the preservation of the records of the main organic organizations in archives of the Wisconsin Historical Society and in a new archive facility on the campus of Western Michigan University where they will be available for researchers who want to learn about the organic movement. But there are also good reasons for a record that is more easily available to a wider range of readers. The organic movement is too important as a social movement to be hidden away in some archive.

To begin with, even as a social movement, organic farming and the food it produces have become a much larger reality than the few farmers who started the movement some forty-five years ago could imagine. This is certainly true in Michigan along with other states that are suitable for the production of food crops. And Michigan was one of the first three states in which farmers' organizations developed standards for the certification of organically-grown food back in the early 1970s, along with Maine and California.

Another reason to publish a book on the organic movement in Michigan is to recognize those who played a leadership role in this new social movement. Farmers have switched from chemical to organic methods for several reasons: because they were concerned about the ecological health of the soil, because they tried to avoid threats to their own health or the health of family members, or to make money. The higher prices for organic produce have been a boon to many smaller organic farmers, and it was well deserved. But the subsequent corporatization of organic farming is distrusted by those who were early adherents in the movement. This distrust has even spawned an organization called Cornucopia, with enough national membership and staff to serve as a watchdog of corporations that tend to flout organic certification standards.

But the most important reason for this book is that organic farming should be recognized as the first step in the recovery of a more ecological and chemical-free method of raising food. Organic farming is growing, and will increasingly grow, because conventional farming has run its course. It was made possible during the last century at a time when the fossil fuel resources for fertilizers and pest control were cheap and easily available. We are now in a time when dependence on those resources is being widely questioned as they pollute our atmosphere with greenhouse gases. And many of the pesticides and fertilizers, according to soil scientists such as Christine Jones in Australia and Elaine Ingham in this country, continue to disrupt and destroy organic matter and humus in the soil. As a result from 50% to 80% of the carbon in the soil has been lost.

The expansion of organic farming, especially regenerative organic farming, will increase levels of organic matter in the soil. In so doing it will help to return the excess of carbon dioxide in the atmosphere to the soils of the earth and thus reduce the speed and power of global warming. The proponents of organic farming are leading in the ways to protect and improve our earth and insure food production in a post-petroleum future. The organic movement is now more important than ever.

The Early Organic Movement in Michigan

Julia Christianson

There were people farming organically in Michigan before the founding of Organic Growers of Michigan in 1973—some who had simply continued to farm in the traditional ways, and others who had been influenced by the writings of European and American proponents of what came to be known as organic agriculture. But there was no statewide organization connecting these farmers, with the exception of the Federated Organic Clubs.

The establishment of Organic Garden Clubs was championed by J.I. Rodale through his magazine *Organic Gardening and Farming* and other publications, beginning in the 1940s. By 1970 over 100 clubs existed across the United States and Canada.

The 1971 edition of *The Organic Directory*, published by Rodale Press, listed 16 clubs in Michigan—Boyne City, Cassopolis, Coldwater, Detroit (2 clubs), Grand Rapids, Grosse Pointe, Hillsdale, Hubbardston, Kalamazoo, Lansing, Monroe, Mt. Morris, Muskegon, Newport, and Williamsburg. The *Directory* singles out two of these clubs:

> Take what happened with one of the newest Organic Gardening Clubs, for instance. Ray McCraney, who operates the all-organic McCraney's Big Hill Farm in Boyne City, Michigan, writes: "We had our first meeting of the Boyne Valley Organic Gardening Club on January 22 of this year. The response in this area was, to say the least, staggering. They turned out over 100 strong on a cold January night. With this type of response we have a great chance of really doing something!"

It goes on:

> **Michigan Clubs in Thick of Efforts.** Elsewhere in Michigan, the Federated Organic Clubs stay in the thick of

efforts to wake up educators and our halls of learning. Federation president E.L. Madsen, who recently took on a DDT-oriented entomologist in a college-sponsored debate, says the statewide groups "are working with students, hoping to induce our large universities to include ecology courses in their curriculum."

One of the Michigan clubs, the very active Tri-County Organic Farm and Garden Club headquartered at Lansing, has been right in the middle of the new drive. At last spring's Earth Day Teach-In at Michigan State University and at other colleges, club folks distributed informative leaflets, took part in the various programs, and got a garden-plot project going with young married couples from the MSU campus.

Tri-County president George W. Haynes, Sr. notes these gardeners took the extra work of weed-clearing the parcel of land in stride last summer, and are "doing a first-rate job." Now, reports the club's Newsletter—mailed to over 300 people—continuing the plots in 1971 is a question to be decided at its first-of-the-year meeting. And some other significant projects and goals:

Shall the Tri-County Club help sponsor the proposed Ecology Center?

Shall we take a more active support of the Eco-Agriculture movement at MSU? These students need us and we need them.

Shall we ask the city of Lansing for space for Organic garden plots for general public use?

Shall we in 1971 handle the sale of beneficial insects and other biological items?

George Haynes of the Tri-County Club took the trouble to travel to Decatur for the first meeting of Organic Growers of Michigan in January, 1973, and offered the Club's support to the new organization.

Long-time organic grower Pat Whetham was a member of the Genesee County club. In the late fall of 2001, she wrote a short article for the newsletter of the Michigan Organic Food and Farm Alliance (MOFFA), excerpts of which appear here:

Continuing A Tradition

In the late 1940's and early 1950's, in response to publications by J.I. Rodale and others, a number of organic farm and garden clubs formed. Five of these clubs banded together to form the Federated Organic Clubs of Michigan in 1953.

From the beginning, the Federated Clubs had a yearly "Round-up" of members which later became the Harvest Festivals. These were held at various locations around the state. The first, in 1953, was held at Ingham County Fairground. There were many important speakers throughout the years, including J.I. Rodale, Robert Rodale, Lady Eve Balfour and Dr. William Albrecht. If you know anything about the history of organic farming and gardening, those names should ring a bell.

I joined the Genesee County Organic Farm and Garden Club in 1980 and attended my first Harvest Festival that year. The one I remember best was in 1981 at Holt High School, where the featured speaker was Robert Rodale. The attendance at that event was very high[1] but it dwindled in the remaining years.

Through the years, the Organic Clubs had some very colorful leaders and members and participated in a number of "causes". In the early 1960's the clubs were involved in lawsuits to combat the spraying of insecticides and have also been involved in fighting such issues as the fluoridation of drinking water.

Many local clubs came and went during the history of the Federated Organic Clubs and the Organic Harvest Festival. When I became involved in 1980 there were 11 active clubs. Today [2001] I think there are at least the remnants of four clubs. Through the years these clubs and their yearly events have offered much in the way of support for organic growing and a less chemical way of life. MOFFA is proud to help continue such a tradition.

While many of the early organic farmers of Michigan were affiliated with one of the Organic Gardening Clubs, the clubs focused more on gardening than farming; they were also active in the forefront of the fight against pollu-

---

[1] Over one thousand people attended, according to a report in the Organic Growers of Michigan newsletter of September, 1981.

tion, as Pat Whetham mentioned in her article quoted above. They were involved in establishing recycling centers, worked to halt aerial spraying programs, promoted municipal composting, and addressed other environmental problems. As the *Organic Directory* notes, in the language of the times, "They're teaming with ecologists, college students, legislators to put more action into the whole environment-action scene." By 1973 the effect of the efforts of the Organic Gardening Clubs and other earth-centered activism had increased the demand for organically grown food and care of the land to the extent that "organic" had undeniably become a "movement."

PART I: OGM

Organic Growers of Michigan, 1973-2005
Maynard Kaufman

Organic Growers of Michigan was organized in southwest Michigan by John and Judy Yaeger, who sent out a note proposing an informal organizational meeting of "organic farmers, fruit growers, and market gardeners" on January 30, 1973. About 40 people attended that meeting in Decatur, Michigan, and began organizing. By March the group had chosen its name: Organic Growers of Michigan Cooperative, Inc. The creation of OGM as a cooperative was deliberate and reflected the cultural importance of cooperation and sharing, including management tasks. This allowed for modest membership dues which started at $7.00 per year and did not go up to $10.00 per year until 1981. By May the certification committee, chaired by Mary Appelhof, was working on certification standards. Six growers were certified "organic" by August of 1973, the first in Michigan through OGM. In this respect OGM was among the leaders in the nation to set up a certification program, along with California and Maine. For more details about the beginnings of the first chapter of OGM the reader is advised to see the article entitled "The Southwest Chapter of OGM" (page 16).

The Yaegers were a fairly young couple who had just begun careers in the Chicago area. Both had their doctorates from the University of Chicago. John was teaching botany and Judy had a position as a researcher in psychology. They had come to southwest Michigan in search of a summer place and started raising vegetables with organic methods. They enjoyed country life so much that in a few years they gave up their jobs in Chicago and moved to their farm, which they called Peacewood. Their effort to organize a group of organic growers was prompted, in part, by their own desire to learn from fellow organic growers. And since the group they initiated was the first group of organic growers for markets in Michigan, they can be recognized as the organizers of Organic Growers of Michigan.

(In 2010 a DVD was made recording a conversation between Judy Yaeger and Maynard Kaufman as they reminisced about the early years of OGM. It is called *The Roots of OGM* and can be seen at http://michiganorganic.org/roots-of-ogm.)

At the October meeting the founding members of OGM approved the by-laws and Articles of Incorporation which were eventually filed with the Department of Commerce in Lansing, with John Yaeger, Mary Appelhof, and Ilda Wissman as incorporators. The by-laws listed four purposes of OGM: to find markets for organic produce, to facilitate the group purchase of supplies, to develop a program and standards for certification of organic produce, and to help educate members and the public about organic issues. The chapters were to be governed by a seven-member executive committee elected by the grower members. By November not only the executive committee but seven other committees were functioning: purchasing, marketing, educational / program, certification, membership, public relations and newsletter. The purchasing committee had already coordinated the purchase and distribution of 180 tons of ground rock fertilizer. And of course the certification committee had done its work. Other committees, such as marketing and public relations, were less effective in Southwest Michigan, but perhaps eventually better in other chapters, such as in the Thumb. The outreach of OGM to the larger farming community was weak. But the internal organization of OGM got off to a great start.

The achievements of the first year reflected the high levels of enthusiasm among members. To prepare for 1974 the treasurer was asked to prepare two budgets: one for 50 members and one for 100 members. In fact the membership roster for 1974 listed 55 grower members and 53 sup-

OGM Field DayGarden Tour, 1998, led by Bruce Shultz at the School of Homesteading

porting members in the Southwest chapter. Supporting members, which included organic gardeners who produced only for household use and people who "believed in" the organic way, were welcome and helpful, but they could not vote or hold office. Grower members included people with as little as one third of an acre to much larger farms who produced for sale. This distinction between growers and supporters was made only after intense and lengthy discussion. The growers for market felt it was necessary to maintain control over certification standards because their economic interests and livelihood were at stake. Livestock was certified separately from land.

When OGM was organized in Southwest Michigan there already were organic gardening clubs, but OGM was the only organic grower group deliberately organized to produce for markets. By April of 1974 another group was organized in the Grand Rapids area, the Grand Valley chapter. (Later, during the 1980s, the group changed its name to the Third Coast chapter.) In any case, the presence of another OGM chapter prompted a revision of the by-laws of the founding Southwest chapter to make provisions for other chapters to form under one set of by-laws. Article Two, on the OGM State Council, was added to the by-laws to facilitate inter-chapter coordination. According to Newsletter #16 (May 1974), the intention was for a state council to meet once a year to coordinate "a system of chapters which allowed for autonomous activity, with little or no bureaucracy forming between the chapters." The early organizers of OGM clearly cherished local control by local groups and did not envision becoming a state-wide political power. Occasionally some members did respond to political issues, but most were reluctant to leave the farm. Later, when the first federal organic standards were released in 1997, OGM was perhaps not adequately prepared to participate as a state-wide organization. But as issues of certification became crucial it turned out that the state council became the main agent of OGM so that the organization could speak with one voice.

Taylor Reid, a perceptive observer of the organic movement, has argued that the back-to-the-land movement of the 1970s helped to shape the organic movement. Certainly parts of it grew out of that back-to-the-land movement with its post-materialistic values. An agrarian environmentalism was emerging which was inclined to disengage from mainstream society and go "back to nature." Many new organic growers sought a more "simple" and self-sufficient way of life as new homesteaders. Others, more concerned about social issues, did attend the annual organic conference during Agriculture and Natural Resources Week at Michigan State University or the Conference in 1984 which included European representatives from IFOAM (International Federation of Organic Agricultural Movements). For a time OGM maintained membership in IFOAM (from 1976 to the early 1980s, and again later in the 1980s), but the dues were expensive and after a few years the membership lapsed.

Earth Day at Bronson Park in Kalamazoo

The first meeting of chapter chairpersons, or State Council, was in March, 1975. Four Chapters were represented: Southwest, Grand Valley, Southeast and Central. These four chapters met again in December, 1975, and agreed to publish a state-wide newsletter. Members of the Grand Valley Chapter edited this newsletter in 1976 and 1977, but it carried news only of the Southwest and Grand Valley chapters. John Yaeger, who had edited the Southwest newsletter during the first three years, resumed that task from 1979 to about 1983, and made an effort to include news from other chapters.

More chapters emerged during these years. A 1977 roster listed members in the Southwest, Southeast, Grand Valley, Central, Thumb Area, and Mid Muskegon Valley Chapters. A 1979 roster included these chapters and the Thornapple and Berrien chapters. The Raisin Valley Chapter functioned during the mid '80s.

OGM membership declined during the decade of the 1980s. Some chapters went dormant or died. Others continued, but even those with many names on the roster had few active members. The Southwest, still the largest with 37 members in 1984, met only sporadically and failed to publish a monthly newsletter in 1984 and 1985. By 1988 OGM consisted of only three active chapters: Southwest, Third Coast (formerly Grand Valley), and Thumb.

The State Council continued to function during these discouraging times. It may have been even more active as a few dedicated members saw the need for strong leadership. Discussions focused on the need for an executive director. Len Prelesnik, from the Third Coast Chapter, volunteered to serve in that capacity from about 1986 to 1988. Lee Purdy, from the Thumb and Lifeline Chapters, succeeded him from 1989 to 1991. These two volunteers did a lot of work for very little if any remuneration, other than expenses, and they helped in the formation of new chapters and the revitalization of old chapters. These included Northwest, Mid-Michigan, Western Upper Peninsula, and Lifeline. Over the years, OGM consisted of at least 13 chapters, but not all were active at the same time. Lee Purdy, as secretary of the State Council, registered the OGM logo with the State of Michigan in 1989. Grey Larison from the Third Coast chapter worked with Lee Purdy and succeeded him in strengthening the State

Council. The work of these volunteers demonstrated the value of an executive director.

The burnout which active volunteers often experience also made the need for a paid executive director more obvious. Overworked OGM members began wishing for a grant or funding to hire staff. Efforts were therefore made in 1989 to revise the by-laws so that OGM could be approved as a charitable organization to which foundations could give tax-exempt gifts. These revisions also strengthened the role of the State Council. Although the bylaw revisions were generally approved by OGM Chapters and by the State Council in November of 1990, some members worried that the transformation of OGM into a charitable and educational organization would inhibit its ability to function on a political level or as a marketing organization. Attorneys also advised that OGM as a business organization would not be likely to receive the 501(c)(3) status from the IRS.

In October of 1991, those OGM members who had been working on the revision of by-laws therefore went ahead, led by Maynard Kaufman and Merrill Clark, to form a new organization. It was incorporated as Michigan Organic Grower Advancement Project, or MOGAP, in January of 1992 and subsequently approved by the IRS as a tax-exempt charitable organization under section 501(c)(3) of the IRS Code. All members of its original board of directors were members of OGM and they sought to coordinate their efforts with the OGM State Council.

Later in 1992 the Board of MOGAP decided to change its name to Michigan Organic Food and Farm Alliance or MOFFA. The board members felt that it was important to emphasize locally-grown food in addition to organic farming. The mission statement adopted by the board reflected this broader concern: "To promote the development of food systems that rely on organic methods of food production and that revitalize and sustain local communities." While MOFFA continued to support OGM and organic agriculture in general, it sought support from a broader range of interest groups by building alliances between growers and eaters of organic food.

As it developed, MOFFA assumed responsibility for some of what OGM had done in the past, especially its educational functions. OGM was left with at least one major responsibility: the administration of its certification program. This had become increasingly important with the

release of the Federal Organic Standards in late 1997. And it had become increasingly difficult and expensive. It took a lot of work for OGM to gain accreditation as a certifying agency under the new federal organic legislation. This chronic concern over issues relating to certification was demoralizing to members who had joined OGM to learn about organic growing. And it was stressful for those who worked on certification issues. Two persons should be recognized who did a lot of this work on certification: Pat Whetham and Grey Larison, who remained the Certification Director for OGM until 2005.

Meanwhile, in 1990 the Organic Foods Production Act was passed by Congress but it was several years before its certification standards were released. When the first standards were released there was widespread opposition from the organic community all over the country. It was the inclusion of three so-called "organic" materials that generated the opposition: sewage sludge, genetically modified organisms, and irradiated foods. Although the organic community was successful in its opposition on this issue, its original enthusiasm for federal standards was dampened. In 1992, when Merrill Clark was nominated and accepted as a member of the first National Organic Standards Board, she was able to report to OGM what she was learning there about the politics of organic food as large industries began producing food that was "certified organic". This was, and remains, a problematic aspect of federal standards.

The process of getting the OGM certification standards and procedures into conformity with the USDA standards and procedures was complex and difficult. Eventually this difficulty and the rising cost of certification fees for growers led to the demise of OGM.

OGM was founded with the expectation that the demand for organically-grown food would increase, that more growers would want to switch to organic methods, and that a local certification program should be in place before federal standards were developed. This has been one of the values of groups like OGM: they set a precedent for the federal standards.

(The author acknowledges with gratitude the information that Taylor Reid made available in his extensive essays and notes on OGM. Judy Yaeger also offered helpful suggestions.)

Chapters of OGM

Organic Growers of Michigan was featured in the December 1973 issue of Rodale's *Organic Gardening and Farming* magazine. In response to this exposure, by March of 1974 OGM was gaining members from all parts of Michigan, some of whom had a desire to become certified. Although the founding members felt an obligation to help these new members achieve certification, travel costs and time for certified members to visit locations outside Southwest Michigan immediately became an issue. The newsletter of March 1974 reported on the situation, and encouraged new members in other parts of the state to find each other through the membership list and organize into regional chapters.

Over the next 30 years, chapters came into existence and dissolved, and sometimes resurrected themselves. By 2002, when the Federal standards for organic certification were finally implemented, six active chapters remained: Southwest, Southeast, Third Coast, Northwest, Lifeline, and Thumb. What follows are the recollections of some of the people who were involved.

Southwest – Maynard Kaufman

The Southwest Chapter of OGM came into being with a typed note on blue-inked ditto paper from John and Judy Yaeger proposing an informal organizational meeting of "organic farmers, fruit growers, and market gardeners" on January 30, 1973. About 40 people attended that meeting in Decatur, Michigan, and began organizing. By March the group had chosen its name: Organic Growers of Michigan, Cooperative, Inc. Six growers were certified "organic" by August of 1973, the first in Michigan through OGM. I am proud to claim that I was one of these six growers on our farm called The School of Homesteading.

(In 2010 a DVD was made recording a conversation between Judy Yaeger and Maynard Kaufman as they reminisced about the early days of OGM. It can be seen at http://michiganorganic.org/roots-of-ogm.)

The Southwest Chapter included members with connections in Chicago, and its proximity to Chicago made that a natural market. But in spite of many meetings designed to enlist growers to ship produce to Chicago, it failed to develop. A few growers responded to the offer of Rick Peshkin, from Frog Holler, near Ann Arbor, to buy organic produce to sell in his area. He did, however, have problems in getting the local farmers to be more careful about how their produce looked. He helped them learn that even organically-grown produce had to be neat and clean. The outreach of OGM to the larger farming community was also weak. But the internal organization of OGM got off to a great start.

In addition to ordering and facilitating the distribution of several boxcar loads of ground rock powders for fertilizer, the Purchasing Committee ordered fish fertilizer and vegetable seeds for distribution to members.

The Southwest chapter of OGM certainly began as a relatively inexperienced group of growers intent on learning about and practicing the best organic growing methods. Only a very few members felt the urgency of political action to challenge and change the way the land grant universities were promoting the use of chemicals in farming. Some did complain about it, but the group as a whole was content to find another more natural way of farming. They also enjoyed getting together with pot-luck meals when meetings included a farm tour, or attending the annual post-Christmas party at the Kaufman home. In its first few years the group was innocently unaware of the difficulties ahead in relation to certification in conformity with the Federal Certification Program.

Other social activities included Field Days which were publicized to attract people who might be interested in organic food and how it is raised. Or a speaker who could attract a crowd was invited, such as Dick Lehnert, then editor of Michigan Farmer Magazine, who was invited to speak at a Field Day for OGM at the School of Homesteading in 1982. But gradually, as the group moved into the decade of the 1980s, it found itself coping with more serious

OGM Field Day at the School of Homesteading, 1978

social issues. One of the first was the attempt to organize protests, along with other environmental groups, against the large-scale spraying of chemicals to kill insect pests such as mosquito or gypsy moth. Several members participated in a large meeting on the MSU campus sponsored by MSU and the International Federation of Organic Agricultural Movements, (IFOAM) in 1984. For several years OGM as a state organization was a member of IFOAM, but dues were expensive and membership was soon discontinued. And of course members attended seminars on farming sponsored by Michigan State University during ANR week, especially after MSU offered special sessions for organic farmers.

The decade of the 1980s was difficult for OGM. The Southwest chapter, still the largest in 1984 with 37 members, met only sporadically and failed to publish a newsletter in 1985. It was resurrected in 1986 through the efforts of Sally Kaufman, who wrote letters to members urging them to get active or decide to disband. This, along with other factors, such as the newsletter edited by Pat Whetham, "Michigan Organic News," helped the group continue. Another factor was the prospect of federal legislation to promote organic food production which was, at least at the outset, enthusiastically welcomed by most organic growers. Still another was the participation of a large grower unit (an 1800 acre cattle farm between Cassopolis and Niles) owned by John and Merrill Clark, who shared their expertise in many meetings of organic growers and eaters in the area.

But in spite of these promising trends and events, many long-time activists in the Southwest chapter of OGM began suffering burnout and wishing for a grant or funding to hire staff. Efforts were therefore made in 1989 and 1990 to revise the by-laws of OGM so that OGM could be approved as a charitable organization to which foundations could give tax-deductible gifts. These revisions also strengthened the state council, since it represented OGM as a unified group. Members of the Southwest chapter were central in this effort and in the subsequent organization of MOFFA (Michigan Organic Food and Farm Alliance) in 1992. Before Sally Kaufman died in 1990, she requested that any memorial gifts be directed to the organic movement, and they did indeed fund the costs of securing IRS 501(c)(3) status for MOFFA.

It was interesting to observe the geographical expansion of the Southwest chapter in the final years of OGM.

While there were still growers in Kalamazoo, Van Buren, Cass and Berrien counties, several more growers emerged in Allegan county, Cinzori Family Farm in Calhoun County, and much further south in Branch county near Coldwater, where Al Weilnau, who served as chair of the Southwest chapter for several years, raised vegetables.

The process of getting the OGM certification standards and procedures into conformity with the USDA standards and procedures was complex and difficult. Eventually this difficulty and the rising cost of certification fees led to the demise of OGM. But its Southwest chapter continued to meet regularly until the end and was in fact growing. Eventually the active growers found other certification agencies.

Third Coast – Fred Reusch

From what I can best remember, it was in the early 1980s after I bought a farm and started "In Harmony Farms" in Rockford and wanted to be a part of a group which could pass knowledge about how to grow organically. The best source of knowledge was from Turtle Island Farm where James DeVries and Charles Bauer had been growing vegetables for a number of years and mostly marketing them at the Grand Rapids Farmers Market. Our initial meetings consisted of our two farms and only 2-3 others depending on the month. We met at the Eastown Food Co-op and mostly discussed growing techniques and getting involved in the Organic Growers of Michigan. I remember Maynard's name as a contact and he may have given us what we had to do to form a chapter.

We soon did what we had to and started a self-certification process. It involved one of our farms visiting another one and writing the required documentation for certification. With so few farms, we regularly went to each other's and it was really a fun, learning event more than checking on each other. Our hearts were so into the organic way that we didn't worry too much about cheating on any of the rules. We also did some group ordering of colloidal phosphate and greensand in 50 lb. bags. We were able to get enough orders to arrange at least part of a truckload. For many years our meetings consisted only of discussing how to solve certain problems we might be having, how to market our produce, and scheduling certification trips.

When the government got involved, we had to get more sophisticated in our certification process. One of our members (I think Grey Larison) took courses so that he could "independently" certify our farms. We also had many discussions about the coming USDA certification process and tried to give as much input as possible. We were now getting up to 7-8 groups coming to meetings although a couple were not farms, but interested in organics. We met at a church for several years—we tried to keep discussions of growing techniques a part of meetings as that was of more interest than the politics. At some point the amount of politics and the dropping of a farm or two caused our small group to disband. It was a fun group but never got big enough to do enough to keep the interest going. We did have a few "local organic days" in late summer in the last few years where we sold produce and tried to educate the public. They did get enough turnout so that we felt it was worthwhile.

I have no records from the years and names are not a specialty of mine, but here is a bit of what I remember:

- Turtle Island Farm – James DeVries and Charles Bauer and crew – veggies
- Carmody Farm – Steve and Kathleen Carmody – blueberries, strawberries, veggies
- N'Harmony Farms – Fred and Mary Reusch – veggies
- Tom and Nancy Zennie – sheep
- Larison Farms – Grey and Judy Larison – veggies
- Len and Ann Prelesnik – some veggies, mostly interest
- Grey Cat Farm – Rich and Sheryl Peterson/Cannon

I'm sure I forgot a few.

Basically we were a small group who were very committed to the organic movement with varied commercial success. Turtle Island was the only farm which made all of their living from farming. I was (and still am) a teacher who had summers and used farming to supplement my income. Steve Carmody was a carpenter which was necessary to keep their farm going. For most of the rest it was more of a hobby. There are several new farms in the Third Coast area that were just getting started as we stopped meeting and I feel our group was at least a starting point where they learned how to get an operation in place.

Fred Reusch is currently a math teacher at Rockford High School. He started an organic restaurant in 1977 (Down to Earth) where he grew many of the vegetables for use in the restaurant. He then ran N'Harmony Farms for 15 years, and continues to support the organic movement.

Southeast – Bob and Linda Kidwell

Using our memories, and a little recorded information, it appears the Southeast Chapter came into existence in 1974. The spark that ignited the formation of the chapter came from a former California union organizer, George Elmendorf, who moved to a small Michigan farm in the area. The early chapter meetings were held in a bank basement in Hudson, MI.

The early meetings were full of great ideas and big plans for a future where there would be an organic grain elevator for marketing members' grain, co-operative marketing of vegetables and meat, co-operative purchasing of supplies, and educational meetings to help the farmers converting to organic. Unfortunately, our inspirational leader left the area, returning to union organizing in California, leaving us to fend for ourselves. We did have a growing membership of farmers and gardeners, mostly the latter. The young, under 30, energetic, "back to the land" crowd from the cities kept things moving along.

In 1976 we came up with the idea of having a field day to educate and help spread the word that OGM-SE existed. The first one was at the Roger and Charlene Hall farm where fertilizing and tillage practices were demonstrated. Bill Mundt from Marcellus, MI was guest speaker. His topic was weed control without chemicals with a focus on buckwheat as a plowdown crop. Attendance was good, but exact figures are lost in the mists of time.

Our one big co-operative purchase was this same year, when we bought a railroad boxcar of colloidal phosphate fertilizer in 50 pound bags through the Fanning Soil Service in Monroe, MI. This large quantity (50 tons?) came directly from the mine in Florida to Montgomery, MI, making shipping cost reasonable. Sometime later another, smaller order was arranged that came by semi. These purchases saturated the market of actual farmers in the group for the time being. We clearly needed more farmers.

In 1977 the field day was at the Bob and Linda Kidwell farm. One hundred and thirty-two attendees signed the registration this year. Maynard and Sally Kaufman were the guest speakers with this year's topic focused on home-steading. Demonstrations of goat hoof trimming, solar water heater construction, spinning, weaving, soap making, and bee keeping went on throughout the day.

In 1978 the field day was held at the Mike and Linda Huraczy farm. Turnout was 111 people, many new faces and addresses to add to our newsletter list. The monthly newsletter was typed on an antique typewriter, and then mimeographed on another old machine. Gene Logsdon was the guest speaker that year and discussed the importance of small farms. Talking to Gene a few years ago, about 2012, he said he and his wife remembered us as a "rather rag-tag group."

In 1979 we had 32 paid family memberships and all was going well. Every month we had a meeting at the Hillsdale high school with speakers on many aspects of organic farming and homesteading. Subjects ranged from agronomy courtesy of Michigan State University Extension service, to raising livestock organically. Sometimes our own members were enlisted to talk about their farms. Members came from a wide area, easily a 40 mile radius, and varied in age from their twenties into their eighties. We had lists of organic crops and meat for sale in case the public desired such things. Who would have guessed it all would stall in a few years? Were we just too far ahead of the national organic movement?

The 1979 field day crowd was only half that of the previous year. And by 1980, with momentum fading, all we managed was a potluck for our members with a field demonstration of plowing and cultivating with horses. This was no longer any kind of outreach activity.

Because attendance at our monthly meetings was falling, and ideas for meeting topics were running short, we divided into sub-chapters to decrease travel distances and allow less formal gatherings at individual farms with an occasional meeting of the entire group. The newsletter kept everyone informed of what was going on where. Burnout was on the horizon. We were looking for a purpose.

The "back to the land", ex-city farmers were discovering farming required a lot of skill, determination, and work. Quietly, some began retreating to their city jobs. By 1981 or 1982, OGM-SE essentially disappeared.

Despite its short life span,[1] the Southeast chapter did serve another purpose that shouldn't be left out. It provided a community where organic growers could connect with others with similar interests. It was good to talk with people who thought organic methods not only were viable, but could be a positive force in agriculture, contrary to the prevailing attitudes in rural Michigan. Many friendships were formed that have lasted nearly four decades.

During the heyday of the Southeast chapter, the Southwest acted, reluctantly, in the role of a state organization. They held state wide meetings on subjects important

---

[1] The Southeast chapter is one of those which dissolved and then re-formed some years later. A new Southeast chapter was formed in 1990-91.

to the entire organization like certification standards. Throughout this period most members felt it was a good idea not to develop a strong central structure for OGM. In 1979 there were seven chapters, each quite independent. Interestingly, the Maine Organic Farmers and Gardeners Association, Maine's equivalent to our OGM, started as we did in 1974, but soon went to a strong central organizational plan. With a grant, they hired one full time employee, who along with a small group of devoted volunteers provided the foundation for the large, successful organic farming group it is today. Perhaps at that time Maine's demographics were enough different from ours to make it possible. It often takes a while for ideas to move from the coasts to the middle of the country.

Bob and Linda Kidwell have owned and operated a diversified organic farm in Hillsdale County since 1974. Now, somewhat retired, they still raise hay, sheep, a large garden, and cut flowers for a farmers market.

Thumb – Joe Scrimger

I shut the combine down early one afternoon in the late summer in good weather to attend the Thumb Chapter of the Organic Growers of Michigan (OGM) meeting in Sandusky, after which I spent 25 years attending monthly meetings for the Thumb OGM and held various officers positions in the organization.

The Thumb Chapter provided a very good social and educational base for growers to get together with like-minded people to share information, concepts and experiences, when the agricultural institutions did not offer much information or encouragement to organic farming in general.

Sid Meyers and Ken Dawson were instrumental in getting the chapter started in the Sandusky area. Later in the 70s Cliff and Bessie Leonard, Lewis and Bea King, Nelson and Ann Davis, along with many others took part in hosting meetings and farm tours when the meetings moved more to the North Branch and Mayville areas. Initially navy beans and wheat were the two crops that were in good demand. Eden Foods was one of the first consistent purchasers of these crops, and they are still purchasing them today.

At the time, Scrimger Farm was more focused on organic freezer beef and sales to stores in Ann Arbor and Detroit, where there was a growing demand. Davis Dairy in Mayville, who ran a 50 cow dairy, probably had one of the first organic dairy farms in the nation, in spite of not having an organic demand at the time for the organic milk in the region. Their milk was sold on the conventional market and for that reason they did not go ahead with certification.

Along the way in the mid 70s, there was communication that started with Dr. Craig Harris in the Sociology Department at MSU and continued with Dr. Thomas Edens from Agriculture and Natural Resources. This evolved to a Sustainable Farming program at Farmer's Week (later called Ag and Natural Resource Week), held in the late winter on campus for the 12-15 years that I worked on as a representative of the Thumb. In the mid to late 80s Dr. Harwood continued the program. From there other programs and contacts with MSU were developed.

The chapter group purchased rail cars of phosphate from Florida and Michigan gravel trains (52 ton) truckloads of lime and gypsum. These were split up where it was needed and used by smaller growers.

We were able to host a tour for the International Federation of Organic Agriculture Movements (IFOAM) at

Scrimger Farm in 1986. The group represented seven to eight different countries. They came all the way from Europe and Australia to look at an organic bean, grain and beef farm operation. It was believed the people from Europe and Australia were also here to visit other farms in the area.

There was a regroup of the chapter in the later 80s to attract more growers for the expanding edible bean and grain markets. The increase in membership was successful but it did slightly change the scope of the Thumb Chapter. This is when there was a need for an international certifier. Out of this Organic Crop Improvement Association (OCIA) was started and the OCIA Michigan #2. Although OGM certification was still being completed, OCIA was starting to get more focus because of the larger acre factor.

Coming back to the growth in bean and grain marketing in the Thumb, another marketing group was developed on a national and international basis, called Organic Farmers of Michigan (OFM) in the fall of 1990. Because of the non-profit nature of OGM, it was felt that this marketing movement, which eventually put a person in Japan to represent our soybeans, should be separated from OGM. This was a good example of a group and businesses that grew out of the Thumb Chapter efforts. Dean Berden of Snover was active in the Thumb Chapter as marketing chairman then continued to work with OFM along with many others from the upper Thumb area.

I started an organic and biological fertilizer and soil testing business that evolved out of the Purchasing Committee of the Thumb Chapter. I worked with farmers who were in transition to organics or who just wanted to reduce their agricultural chemical use. I still do soil testing today and have downsized the farm from 500 to 100 tillable acres which are currently done on shares by another "new" organic farmer. The Thumb Chapter fostered other business growth in such ways.

Randy Hampshire from the Kingston area was originally involved with the chapter while operating a 100 cow dairy operation. Later he worked with the marketing groups, sold the dairy and built a wood fired brick oven to bake bread for the regional market. Randy and Shirley are still baking today and have added a "cow share" fresh milk enterprise to the farm, along with vegetable production that is marketed in the Detroit Farmers market, and in Oakland County. Hampshire Farm is an exceptional example of production from the soil, to the wheat, to the bread, and then to the consumer, that is shared with many others through apprenticeships and training programs.

Another example of what impact the Thumb chapter had on farming in the Thumb, is that there currently exists what was the largest contiguous block of organic farms in the Midwest, at over 10,000 acres. These farms are located just north of Caro, in the middle of the Thumb. This is mostly made up of larger (1000+ acre) bean and grain farms that started after one of these farmers attended a Thumb OGM tour. This growth, along with most rapid double digit growth, brought opportunity along with other issues to the makeup of the chapter. Add to that, the demand for organic soybeans outpaced most other bean and grain demand in the 1990s, reducing some of the diversity that the chapter had. At that time it was discussed that it might have been easier to milk the soybeans than the cows. However, in the long term, this discussion proved to be false as organic dairy certainly has its place in the market. It will take many opinions and years to determine how this affected the chapter in the long term.

After 25 years of monthly meetings I decided it was my time to move on. Les Roggenbuck of Snover, Chuck Herpolsheimer of Imlay City, John Simmons of North Branch, and many others kept the chapter going for many years in its "hay days" of growth in the new century. At this time an administrator was hired for the chapter.

In the years since then, the regional co-op elevator just purchased one of the other bean and grain marketing groups that evolved out of the Thumb Chapter. We are not sure if that means part of the system has run full circle; only time will tell.

It is for sure that the Organic Growers of Michigan Cooperative Inc. and the Thumb Chapter have affected Agriculture in our state. I hope that MOFFA is able to keep the best of this legacy to carry on in the expanding local/regional food movement and organic production in general, which in my terms may more fully express some of the original organizational intent of the Thumb Chapter of the Organic Growers of Michigan.

Joe and Kay Scrimger started farming organically in 1973 and by 1975 had transitioned 280 acres to an organic program. They were OGM members from 1976 to 2002; Joe was Thumb Chair and State Chair along with other positions. Scrimger Farm now has 130 acres and is certified by OCIA.

Lifeline – Linda Purdy with help from Lee Purdy

In my memories of the Lifeline Chapter it was a really great organization when I was there in the early to mid 1990s. The group met in churches and in the homes of members. At the first meeting I attended several members were just about to give up, but they persevered and became a new family for me. I particularly remember Bob and Eleanor Glick just west of Perry. Coming from Detroit I assumed that rural people were cliquish and probably somewhat racist. But when Eleanor showed me her newsletter from the Southern Poverty Law Center, which monitors hate groups and fights racism, she changed those attitudes in me.

An interesting aspect of this chapter is its name. It started in about 1988 and was called Lifeline because it connected the Third Coast chapter in the west to the Thumb chapter in the east. Members were scattered in Clinton, Shiawassee, Genesee, Eaton, Ingham and Livingston counties. Because of the long distances between members, attendance at meetings was probably about 8 to 15 out of a total membership of around 20 to 25.

Officers in our chapter were rotated on a regular basis. Among the people who chaired the group was Lee Purdy who was also State Secretary at the time and helped other chapters, such as Mid-Michigan, Northwest, and Upper Peninsula, get started. Other officers and leaders included Craig Howard, Jane Bush, Sue Houghton, Linda Purdy, and Gene Purdum, who, along with Pat Whetham, were leaders in our chapter and in OGM on the state level where Pat was State Certification Director.

Our members were active in a wide variety of enterprises. Chuck Haynes in Lansing did some sort of urban gardening thing; Pooh Stevenson just west of Owasso had a CSA, Rob Malcomnson from Davison raised vegetables, as did Dale Kunkle, Patti Travioli, Lynn Meisner, and Tim and Robyn Leonard. Then there was Richard Ferris, the miller, Luttenbacher Greenhouse in Clio, and Andrew and Nancy Sloan who had an organic plant nursery. I had a certified organic herb farm called Sun Dances Garden. Before I married Lee he was raising beef and grain at Westwind Farm.

As I write this I keep remembering more of the wonderful people in our chapter. There were Harley and Linda Thomas, Tom and Lynn Bowden, and Frank and Kay Jones, all from Shiawassee County. Bill Vondrasek was from Bath, and Genesee County had James Buchanan and John Chaprnka.

We did a lot of fun social things. To celebrate the harvest we often had a tomato tasting contest at the homes of different members or a cherry tomato spitting contest. We also had potluck meal at which people brought produce from their gardens. Bob Glick always brought a goose near Thanksgiving, which was new to me and took some getting used to. We had guest speakers, and one of the best I remember was Joe Scrimger on weeds and what they tell us about soils. We also heard Phil Wheeler, who was very chemistry-oriented and scientific.

The downfall of the group, I believe, is that every meeting ended up being a debate over national certification, and whether or not the federal government should be involved. Once in a while, we'd get really great presentations, like the one by Joe Scrimger just mentioned, or our annual post harvest dinner, which was great fun, but more often than not, it was pro- v. anti-government involvement. We know what happened (I was pro) and now, I think organic farming may have been better off left alone. One of our members, Steve Grose, argued that we should stay with our own group and not get involved with the federal program. At that time I was actually saying that national certification would be better because it would be consistent and people would see the logo and know exactly what it meant. But of course he was correct as the big corporate people got involved in that. At any rate, we may be back to the old ways before you know it with the current administration.

I would like to see another, similar, group form again. OGM's Lifeline Chapter was a great support system for organic growers. It was a very significant factor for 12 to 15 years, and continued to function about as long as OGM continued. As I remember the folks in the organic movement, I will say that one thing we don't have now that

OGM gave us was a *community of growers,* all with really the same frame of mind, despite minor differences. I am so glad I got to be a part of all this, and hope that we can all work together again in the future.

Lee and Linda met at an Organic Growers of Michigan meeting in the spring of 1994; it was Linda's second Organic Growers meeting. Lee had been raised at Westwind Farm, and had just moved back with his two young daughters; Linda had a certified organic herb farm. When they got together, they had both been looking at an historic flour mill in Argentine which had been up for sale for several years. They bought it together, got married, and tried to combine two families, all at the same time, in 2000-2001. They were millers of certified organic grains for 15 years. In 2016, they sold the Mill, and are now readying their stone mill to be up and operating in its new location at Westwind Farm—while growing their own grain, operating a CSA, hosting educational, sustainable living events, and participating in online sales of all their farm products.

Before turning to the next article, which recounts the final years of OGM, it may be helpful to bear in mind that OGM started as a group of regional chapters that were very socially oriented. As you read the following article by Pat Whetham you will understand how these regional chapters were cut off from OGM as it was transformed into a certifying agency. Thus only five of the thirteen chapters could be persuaded to send us a report on their chapter.

The Organic Certification Program After National Organic Standards

Pat Whetham

Late in 1997 the USDA finally released for public comment the proposed "organic rule". This was published in the Federal Register, as are all proposed rules from the federal government. A number of meetings for public comment were set up and comments were accepted online.

A review of this proposed rule showed many, many inconsistencies with the organic standards used across the country. But the leaders of Organic Growers of Michigan were also reviewing the rule's requirements for organization and for acceptance, inspection, and review of applicants for organic certification. OGM had always been organized in a chapter system and each chapter had managed certification application, inspection and review in a specific area of the state. Our understanding of the proposed organic rule indicated that this chapter system would no longer work.

OGM meetings, both chapter and state, had often been long, argumentative discussions about what could and could not, should and should not be included in our organic standards. This was true of many organic certification groups around the country. The difference in standards from state to state was always an issue for buyers of organic crops. The Organic Foods Production Act passed in 1990 gave us some hope for a nationwide standard that would help us in the marketplace. But first there must be a standard we could agree upon. Up until the publication of that first proposed rule, it had not really occurred to members or leadership of OGM that the chapter system would not work. Faced with changes not just to the standards but also to the structure of our organization, the state council announced a meeting of all chapters to discuss the necessary adjustments to our certification system.

OGM gathered for the meeting in January, 1998. Prior to this day only a few phone discussions had been held on the subject of changing the way we certified farms. A number of OGM members had attended a training week for inspectors held in April 1996 and through that had a bit more insight into larger certification organizations. These people were asked to attend this meeting, along with OGM chapter officers and any interested members. Changes were proposed as the group read and discussed the requirements laid out in the proposed organic rule. Clearly, changes were in order and through the sometimes heated discussion the necessary adjustments were agreed upon.

It was decided that OGM would not abolish the chapters but separate from them. The OGM state council became the certification body and a Certification Director was named, as well as a committee to bring OGM up to the requirements of the Organic Rule. After this some OGM chapters dissolved. Others continued as separate but connected educational groups, continuing to meet the educational needs of members as well as interested growers and consumers.

The Certification Committee worked for several months to create the new system, with new organic farm plan questionnaires, inspection forms and procedures, review documents, etc. Training sessions were planned so OGM had enough inspectors to avoid conflicts of interest. The growing season in 1998 was the first implementation of the new system for OGM, although the standards used were still old since the USDA had yet to finalize a rule.

The USDA received more comments on this proposed rule than any in its history, topping out at well over a quarter million comments online—most of them opposed. The talking sessions held around the country brought out many growers and consumers who made their desires and  fears known. Although the organizational structures laid out in this first proposed rule didn't change much, there were significant changes in standards that showed up in the second proposed rule and in the final rule. The final organic rule went into effect in 2002. The final rule excluded the "big three" issues from the first proposed rule: genetically modified organisms, sewage sludge use and irradiation.

OGM continued to adapt as much as possible and passed the initial audit from the USDA. But as requirements tightened leading up to a second, more stringent audit, it didn't look good for the continuation of OGM as an organic certification organization.

By this time (early to mid-2000s) most of us were online and could see and be part of greater discussions that included other certifiers across the country. It was clear that the second round of audits was brutal, even for well-funded and professionally staffed larger certification organizations. Conflict of interest and separation from "education" were still major problems. OGM sent out a letter of explanation and a questionnaire to all certified members and called a meeting for early in 2006. Could we make the necessary changes? Would the growers be willing to pay more for certification so that OGM could pay professional staff? Could we pay the charges from the USDA for the audit? And a number of other questions.

This meeting came with a distinct lack of interest from the certified producers of OGM. All were well aware of the other certifiers available to them, even though at greater cost. No one seemed to have the energy to continue as an organic certification body. We voted to discontinue organic certification. We gave up our USDA accreditation as of March 1, 2006.

An additional meeting was held later in March to see if there was any interest in continuing Organic Growers of Michigan as a purely educational and social organization. Again, the question was met with a near total lack of interest. A vote was taken and OGM officially dissolved, to the sorrow of many.

Pat Whetham has been gardening organically since the mid-70s and joined the Genesee County Organic Farm and Garden Club in 1980. Upon the dissolution of the Federated Organic Clubs in 1986, she took over as editor of Michigan Organic News, which continued as a stand-alone publication. Pat was a founding board member of MOFFA and served as Vice Chair for a number of years. She was also active in Organic Growers of Michigan beginning in the mid-1980s, and served as Organic Certification Director from 1998 - 2000 and 2005 - 2006. She farms with her husband at Whetham Organic Farm, Inc. in Flushing, Michigan. The farm has been certified organic since 1988, raising mostly field crops but also organic vegetables. For the past 13 years the farm has also run a small CSA.

PART II: MOFFA

Origins of Michigan Organic Food and Farm Alliance (MOFFA) [1]

Maynard Kaufman

The origins of MOFFA, Michigan Organic Food and Farm Alliance, are part of the history of Organic Growers of Michigan, (OGM). OGM grew rapidly during the 1970s to eight or nine chapters, but interest declined during the 1980s when the organization became dependent on a few active leaders rather than on member participation. As these volunteer leaders suffered burnout from overwork, the need for a paid executive director became obvious. Therefore, in 1989 and 1990, some of the leaders, primarily Merrill Clark and I, began work on changing the OGM by-laws so that OGM could be recognized as a charitable organization and receive grants to hire an executive director.

In summer of 1991 I discussed these efforts with Lynne Blahnik and Ed Marks who had recently returned to Michigan after working with the North American Farm Alliance, which Ed, an attorney, had served as executive director. I was advised that OGM as a business coop would not likely receive the 501(c)(3) status from the Internal Revenue Service. In October of 1991, those OGM members who had been working on the revision of by-laws called a meeting to form a new organization. Legal costs and the

---

[1] This article covers the period from the founding of MOFFA in 1991 through 2004. The chapters "MOFFA in the '90s: Enlarging the Organic Movement in Michigan" and "MOFFA in the 21st Century" cover other aspects of the organization during this time and in later years.

IRS filing fee were provided by a memorial fund of $1,255 in honor of my late wife Sally who had requested that OGM be designated to receive memorial gifts.

The new organization was called Michigan Organic Grower Advancement Project (MOGAP). It was incorporated in the state of Michigan in January of 1992 and was approved by the IRS as a tax-exempt charitable organization under section 501(c)(3) of the IRS Code in June of 1992. The incorporators were Maynard Kaufman, Pat Whetham and Grey Larison. Since I had called the organizational meetings I assumed the chair. Pat Whetham agreed to serve as vice chair, Merrill Clark as secretary, and John Valenti as treasurer. Other charter board members included Laura DeLind and of course Grey Larison. All board members were members of OGM and efforts were made to schedule MOGAP board meetings on the same day and place as the meetings of the State Council of OGM. (See Appendix B for a list of MOFFA board members and officers.)

Lynne Blahnik, who had been watching the board from the sidelines, recognized that board members needed leadership training. In May of 1993 she offered to lead in strategic planning and the board accepted her offer. After a couple of marathon sessions in June and September, board members were clearer about how they wanted the organization to develop. The name was changed to Michigan Organic Food and Farm Alliance (MOFFA) and a mission statement was adopted to reflect the broader concerns of the organization: "MOFFA promotes the development of food systems that rely on organic methods of food production and that revitalize and sustain local communities." These actions represented a shift away from OGM. In part this reflected the board's perception that OGM as an organization had been less than fully cooperative, and the fact that few OGM members supported MOFFA. But the main reason for the shift away from OGM was the board's broader concern for the development of local organic food systems, which include but are more than organic agriculture. Various board members, and especially Laura DeLind, had been arguing that MOFFA should move beyond the commercial aspects of organic farming toward a consideration of social and ecological issues. MOFFA's "local food" logo, which was created by Laura DeLind, was made available for MOFFA's use during this time.

At the conclusion of the strategic planning sessions, Lynne Blahnik offered to serve as executive director of MOFFA with the expectation that she could secure at least most of the funds for her salary from grants. The board welcomed this offer and approved it in September. Unfortunately, Lynne had to terminate this arrangement when she moved out of state later in fall.

In March of 1994 the board, with a grant of $10,000 from Michigan Land Trustees, (see Appendix C for a list of grants received by MOFFA), hired Judith Pedersen-Benn as executive director on a half-time basis. She continued Blahnik's work on internal organization and served as contact person for MOFFA until she resigned on Dec. 1 of 1994 to take a full time position. Administrative duties were then divided among board members, an arrangement which continued for several years.

Over the years MOFFA has been engaged in a number of projects and activities. One of the first of these was the publication of a bi-monthly newsletter. Early in 1992 Pat Whetham offered the periodical she was editing for the organic community, *Michigan Organic News*, as a MOGAP newsletter and the board accepted her offer. Beginning with the May-June issue in 1994, Laura DeLind began editing a new newsletter, *Michigan Organic Connections,* as MOFFA's newsletter. She continued as editor until late in 1995 when April Allison, who had been helping her, became editor and continued until the end of 1999. Pat

Whetham served as editor throughout 2000 and early in 2001 a newsletter committee consisting of Gail Campana, Merrill Clark, and Pat Whetham assumed responsibility for the newsletter, with Merrill as managing editor, a position she held through 2002. Pat Whetham began serving as editor in 2003.

Since MOFFA originated as the "educational arm" of OGM, it was fitting that MOFFA assumed responsibility for the "organic day" program at the annual Agriculture and Natural Resources (ANR) Week at Michigan State University. With her position on the faculty at MSU, Laura DeLind was in a position to coordinate this program for MOFFA and did so from 1993 through 1997. She provided nationally-known speakers and coordinated the workshops each year and served as informal advisor through 1999 as other board members worked with Michigan State University Extension (MSUE) people to coordinate the Organic Day program. In 2001 the Michigan Department of Agriculture (MDA) planned and funded a very special program in recognition of the adoption of federal standards for organically grown produce. During the next two years board members worked with MSUE staff people to plan and present the programs.

A major project, intended to be an annual event, was the organization of the Michigan Organic Harvest Festival. Each Festival required the contacting of growers and exhibitors, the acquisition of funds, planning a program and making arrangements for a place. The first one, in 1995, was at the Washtenaw Community College near Ypsilanti. In 1996 it was at the Fowlerville Fairground, in 1997 at the Ingham County Fairground, and in 1999 again at the Washtenaw Community College. The Harvest Festival was so demanding, given the limited personnel and resources MOFFA had to work with, that it could not be done every year. Board members who worked especially hard on the Festival include Betty Edmunds, who also handled financial matters, Pat Whetham, Merrill Clark, Susan Houghton and Sharon Renier, along with MOFFA members who volunteered.

In 2001 Lisa Wesala and her colleagues in Healthy Traditions Network worked with MOFFA to organize a Harvest Festival in the Detroit area. She continued that Festival in 2002 and 2003. During these years another Festival was organized in the Grand Rapids area by Grey Larison and the Third Coast chapter of OGM. In 2003 these Festivals were joined by a third in the Kalamazoo area organized by Maynard Kaufman with help from food and farming groups in Southwest Michigan. This Harvest Fest meets at Tillers International near Scotts, Michigan, east of Kalamazoo, and eventually Tillers "owned" it and is the main sponsor. Regional Harvest Festivals have provided a vital context for the organization of local groups and local food systems.

George Bird and Pat Whetham at the Harvest Festival in Grand Rapids, 2003

Another major project has been the publication of *Eating Organically: A Guide to Michigan's Organic Food Producers and Related Businesses*. This project was initiated and edited by Laura DeLind who included not only the rosters of growers but also short articles on various topics related to organic food, farming and related issues. Laura edited the 1995, 1996-97, and 1999 editions. Susan Smalley, of MSUE, and Pat Whetham assisted with the 1999 edition. Providing for adequate sales and distribution of the directories was an on-going problem. The 1999 edition was totally underwritten by MSUE. Jim Bingen, Suzanne Smucker, Nancy Keiser and Pat Whetham prepared a shorter directory, without articles, for publication in 2003; it was updated and published again in 2008. In 2013 the guide was brought online so it can be updated continuously, and a paper edition was made available once again beginning in 2015.

Other publications by MOFFA during this period included a brochure to solicit members, a brochure on food terms called "Food for Thought," a brochure called "Pesticides and Children," and a brochure called "What is Organic?".

In addition to specific projects, MOFFA board members carried on continuous activities such as maintaining relationships with environmental organizations, maintaining contacts with organic grower groups, keeping up with and testifying on legislative issues relevant to organic food and farming, staying in touch with sister organizations such as Michigan Integrated Food and Farming Systems (MIFFS), Michigan Agricultural Stewardship Association (MASA), and others, along with cultivating relationships with MSU personnel. MOFFA was also of assistance as MDA worked on the development of state organic standards.

Not all of MOFFA's projects have been successful. A rental library of videos on organic food and farming failed because of insufficient demand. A speakers bureau, which was announced in 1997, received few if any requests for speakers. Board members have, of course, been asked to speak on various topics over the years, but seldom on the topics listed. Another project which could claim limited success was designed to recognize an "organic farmer of the year" or a "local food award" for a group or individual. MOFFA did, however, give out awards for several years: "Lifetime Achievement", "Public Service", "Community

Service", and "Volunteer of the Year" awards. A list of awards given by MOFFA may be found in Appendix D.

In a series of strategic planning meetings led by Pat Whetham in 1998 and 1999, board members agreed that MOFFA should promote not only the demand for organic food but also the supply of organic food produced and processed in Michigan. One important step toward this end was the use of MDA "Risk Management" funds to provide for a MOFFA presence at the Great Lakes Fruit and Vegetable Expo in Grand Rapids, in an effort to encourage conventional growers to transition to organic methods.

As an organization recognized by the IRS under section 501(c)(3) of its code, MOFFA is eligible to receive tax-deductible grants from corporations, foundations and governmental agencies, and much effort was expended in writing grant proposals. In spite of these efforts, no major grants were received from large foundations during this period. Proposals to governmental agencies have been more successful. Although grants received by MOFFA are listed in Appendix C, some deserve special mention in that they reflect the range of MOFFA's activities.

The mobile processing trailer at Ware Farm, 2003

Susan Houghton was successful with a proposal to the USDA Sustainable Agricultural Research and Education Program (SARE) for funding of over $41,000 to build a mobile processing trailer. It was originally hoped that the trailer could be used for catering organic food, but provisions of the grant required it be used first for educational demonstrations, such as on-farm processing. From 1999 to

2015 the trailer was leased by various organic growers to add value by processing some of their produce.

In 1998, Laura DeLind received a grant from SARE of almost $24,000 to make a survey of Community Supported Agriculture (CSA) programs in Michigan, Ohio and Indiana. Her findings were summarized in a book, *The Many Faces of Community Supported Agriculture*, published by MOFFA.

Thanks to the cooperation and advice from people supportive of organic food and farming at MSU, especially Richard Harwood and John Fisk, and to MSU Extension, MOFFA was named as grantee of a fund of about $70,000 for a program of on-farm research projects over the years from 1998 to 2001. This helped to provide good publicity and higher visibility for MOFFA along with some funds for a computer needed to carry out its programs.

As the organic "industry" became regulated by federal and state legislation for certification standards and procedures, MOFFA, as Michigan's only organic advocacy group, gained recognition from the Michigan Department of Agriculture, especially through Chris Lietzau's efforts in the Department of Agricultural Development in the MDA. The ANR Week Conference on Organic Agriculture in March of 2001, which was planned and supported by MDA, testified to those efforts. MOFFA, which advised on nationally-known speakers, was one of the sponsors.

The very fact that organic food was becoming an "industry", however, raised questions for many long-time organic growers and advocates. Some felt that recognition by governmental agencies was the kiss of death. As large food corporations began to buy or control the organic industry, and as they pressured the USDA for standards favorable to their enterprise, a kind of counter-movement emerged. As growers became disillusioned with corporate control and higher certification fees, the number of certified organic growers diminished. Therefore in 2004 the MOFFA Board began to question whether to emphasize local food more than organic food and even encourage eaters toward local food even though it might not be "certified organic".

Board members were hopeful that increased recognition of MOFFA would help in securing funding for professional staff to carry out its programs. New projects for which to seek foundation funding were under consideration. Increased recognition did seem to help in attracting members to MOFFA. By 2001 membership had grown to about 200, and by 2004 it was about 230. Membership fees and large donor gifts provided for almost all of MOFFA's administrative expenses. Occasional profit from sale of goods, such as publications, posters, t-shirts and tote bags, and profit from harvest festivals or similar events also contributed to working capital.

MOFFA in the '90s: Enlarging the Organic Movement in Michigan

Laura B. DeLind

During the 1980s and early 1990s organic agriculture in the U.S. was principally the concern of organic producers and organic specialists. It was a time, oddly enough, when despite differing philosophies, the organic movement shared a good deal in common with conventional agriculture. Organic agriculture may have been about building living soils and working with natural processes while conventional agriculture may have been about dissecting and overriding nature to push scale and efficiency, but both were focused almost exclusively on the hard science of production.

Early organic farming conferences were myopic affairs, largely about the experience of farming. Equipment was discussed, techniques were compared, research was reported, certification standards were reviewed, and strategies for selling organic 'product' were presented. There was not yet a sense that what was being raised was food, or that food was something other than a commodity. The significance of food and its ability to bridge time and place, to have sociocultural as well as natural dimensions, and to connect empirical and spiritual realities was still missing from most organic conversation. The number of women farmers (as well as opportunities for women in agriculture) could be counted on one hand. Little attention was paid to the needs and capacities of eaters (i.e., the non-farming population). Likewise, the value of aesthetics and the role of the humanities in food and farming were conspicuous only by their absence. For all its alternative-ness the organic movement had not fully embraced the notion of diversity or of whole systems thinking.

This was the mind-set that MOFFA knew best when it first began to promote the organic movement in Michigan. It was also the mind-set it would challenge. The original MOFFA Board was an unusual mix of men and women— philosophers, farmers, social scientists, and political activists—who struggled to find a language to address their common belief that the agrifood system was deeply flawed and that organically-based alternatives were absolutely necessary. They wanted to support Michigan's organic producers but they also wanted to expand the notion of organic to include a way of living, of thinking and being. This meant moving beyond their individual comfort zones. It meant allowing ideas like 'eater' and 'community' and 'place' to co-exist with 'soil biota,' 'natural sprays,' and 'price points.'

MOFFA logo created by Laura B. DeLind, 1994

To this end, one of MOFFA's first initiatives was to take on the responsibility for organizing a public program during what was called "ANR Week" (Agriculture and Natural Resources Week), held annually on the Michigan State University campus during spring break. These programs were designed to promote organic food and farming throughout the state and to educate both organic farmers and those who saw organics as an instrument for social and political change. Early programs were two days long and were organized around keynote speakers, workshops and locally-sourced organic meals. They also deliberately invited women speakers, showcased new concepts (e.g., co-ops, community-supported agriculture, city composting, farmer-hospital alliances), and included artful forms of expression (e.g. song, theater).

Over the course of the first five years, George Siemon spoke about Organic Valley, Wisconsin's farmer-owned dairy cooperative. Ken Taylor spoke about his work politically organizing eaters in Minneapolis/St. Paul. Dana Jackson spoke about landscape and biodiversity. Elizabeth Henderson spoke about her work with Community Supported Agriculture. Kent Whealy spoke about his work with Seed Savers Exchange and the value of heirloom seed. Joan Gussow spoke about organic standards in the context of real nutrition. Jack Kloppenburg Jr. spoke about corporate control of the food supply. Odessa Piper spoke about her restaurant L'Etoile, and the sourcing, preparing, and serving of organic foods.

One evening, Kaiulani Lee presented her acclaimed one-woman play, "A Sense of Wonder," honoring the life and work of Rachel Carson. On another evening, writer Stephanie Mills read from her essay on bioregionalism. All of these programs were attended by hundreds of people. All pushed the organic agenda into new conceptual territory. They helped to catalyze new partnerships between farmers and eaters and community institutions across the state. Over the years, these partnerships have continued to grow, extending the reach of organics and the organic movement into larger debates around food democracy and food security for Michigan and the nation.

Bringing organic farmers and eaters and local institutions together was also central to MOFFA's organic, statewide directory, *Eating Organically*. The first edition (also the first in Michigan) was published in 1995 under the editorship of board member Laura B. DeLind. Organized by county, the directory profiled organic, transitional, and non-certified farmers as well as organic businesses (e.g. bakeries, mills, stores), giving greater visibility to these enterprises. Yet, the early directories were far more than perfunctory listings of people and products. Rather, they were artfully designed with graphics and essays written largely by MOFFA's board members on dozens of food and

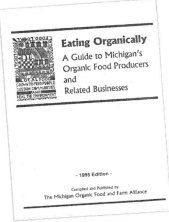

farm-related topics. There were essays on canning and lacto-fermentation, on understanding food terminology, and on environmental stewardship. There were songs and poems and personal memoirs. Altogether, the intent was to illustrate in multiple ways the vast nature of what an organic life entailed and what it had to offer.

This was the spirit that pervaded the early days and programs of MOFFA. It was a young organization of talented, opinionated and energetic people. They argued, they wrote, they researched, and they led by example. They were intent on finding ways to support organic growers and to inform and invite the general public to take part in the fullness of the organic movement.

Dr. Laura B DeLind was a founding board member of MOFFA. She edited MOFFA's first organic directory and coordinated MOFFA's ANR programs for many years. She was instrumental in establishing Growing in Place Community Farm, a CSA that operated from 1995-2002. In 2010, she co-founded and continues to direct the Lansing Urban Farm Project, a 501(c)(3) organization whose mission is to raise and market fresh produce on Lansing's Eastside, train urban farmers, and promote urban agriculture.

MOFFA in the 21ˢᵗ Century

Jim Bingen

As MOFFA knocked on the door of the 21st Century, the organic movement throughout Michigan was alive, well, and prepared for a bright future. After more than 10 years of frustratingly slow progress, the National Organic Program was on the cusp of being launched, and the State of Michigan was rolling out its own program to support and promote organic farming and marketing.

MOFFA, OGM and the NOP

In his chapter "Organic Growers of Michigan, 1973-2005," Maynard Kaufman discusses the decision in the early 1990s by several OGM members to create MOFFA as a means to broaden and popularize a statewide platform for organic food production that would "revitalize and sustain local communities." Regular reports about, and announcements for OGM, including the list of officers and regional chapters, in the *Michigan Organic Connections* newsletter reflected this close relationship until the demise of OGM early in the new century.

By the late 1990s, Merrill Clark, one of the founders of MOFFA, was deeply involved in developing the national organic standards, and she provided regular updates on the halting steps toward implementation of the National Organic Program. However, when the NOP was finally launched in 2000, the Michigan organic community was not wildly enthusiastic. OGM received conditional accreditation as a certifying agency from the USDA in 2003, but ultimately was unable to meet the NOP requirements. Moreover, many Michigan organic growers were deeply concerned about the "bureaucratization" of organic practices and the loss of organic values and ethics in the new national standards. After waiting for over 10 years, the Michigan organic community was reticent about embracing the national standards.

Pat Whetham, MOFFA member, former Vice President of OGM, former organic inspector, and farmer, summed up the concerns: given the influence of big money in the implementation of the national organic standards, "those of us seeking a truly clean, safe, organic food supply are unlikely to find foods we can trust.... Local markets for locally grown organic foods become more important than ever."

MOFFA, the Michigan Organic Products Act and the Michigan Department of Agriculture

While Michigan organic growers were skeptical of the national standards and could not meet the conditions to register OGM as a certifying agency, MOFFA's relationships with the Michigan Department of Agriculture during the early years of the 21st century were very collaborative and productive. In March 1998, the MDA convened a one-day meeting to discuss the OFPA (Organic Foods Production Act) and to solicit comments from the Michigan organic farming community that would be shared with the USDA. As Merrill Clark reported, the MDA was making an effort to create new connections with the state's organic growers. Some of these new connections included: the creation of the MDA Organic Registry to help protect organic growers from pesticide drift; participation in some of the meetings of the National Organic Standards Board; an invitation to MOFFA to join the MDA booth at the Michigan State Fair; and, a proposal to establish an organic food advisory committee of growers, processors, handlers, retailers and consumers that would develop a strategic plan for advancing the Michigan organic foods industry.

In October of 2000, the Governor signed the Michigan Organic Products Act in order "to define organic agriculture and products [and] to provide for the establishment of standards relative to organic products, producers and handlers of organic product." In March of the following year, the MDA sponsored the first Michigan Organic Conference. This landmark event was held at the MSU Kellogg Center and co-chaired by MOFFA members Merrill Clark and Carol Osborne.

The Expanding Organic Movement

Without question, passage of the Michigan Organic Products Act built upon the growing, and truly grassroots organic movement around the state. The Organic Harvest Festivals had been started in the mid-1990s, and often included nationally known leaders in the U.S. organic community. Representing the strength of the state's organic grain growers in the Thumb area, the Michigan Farmer's Union launched the Organic Tofu Cooperative in 1998. The Michigan Organic Dairy Group was organizing, and Westwind Milling opened in 2000.

An Organic Growers Forum was held in 2001, and in the same year the Healthy Traditions Network held its first Growing Connections Festival. MOFFA participated in each of these annual festivals for several years, as well as other festivals around the state, including the Wheatland Music Festival.

MOFFA and MSU/MSUE

Following its involvement in two SARE grants, one on soil fertility and field testing and another to establish a network of cooperative organic supporters in order to lay the framework for additional organic support in Michigan, in 1999 MOFFA collaborated with OGM, OCIA, and the

MSU Agricultural Experiment Station (AES) to manage an On-Farm Research and Demonstration Program.

An organic apple production study was launched at the Clarksville MSU Research Station in 2000, and in 2001, the MSU Project GREEEN continued to fund this research. In 2002, a Northport cherry producer started to test the efficacy of organic pest management for Michigan cherries.

MOFFA hosted an "Organic Day" with MSU as early as 1997, and in 1999 helped to sponsor the MSU/ANR Week on Sustainable Agriculture with a program on "The Value of Eating Locally" by Dick Lehnert. In 2002, MSU hosted a meeting with growers on organic farming research and sponsored a visit by three MSU faculty members to the Swiss Organic Agriculture Research Institute, FIBL. That same year, MOFFA and OGM members were asked to submit research ideas for the MSU Extension research Project GREEEN. Laura DeLind, of MSU and MOFFA, worked closely with Terry Link, Director of Campus Sustainability, on a campus-wide coordinating committee for a "sustainable campus" that involved trying to make local and organic food available in two MSU residence halls. John Clark, a member of both OGM and MOFFA, supplied over 500 pounds of certified organic beef to this program.

As noted above (and by Maynard Kaufman in his chapter on MOFFA in this book), during the early 2000's there were several relatively close, collaborative efforts between MSU, MSUE, MOFFA and the MDA. In 2002, the Dean of the MSU College of Agriculture asked MOFFA to participate in an evaluation of the current status of organic research in the college, and specifically to make recommendations for ways to enhance this research at MSU. In 2003, MDA provided a $20,000 Risk Management grant to MOFFA in order to support workshops, conference exhibits, organic field days and other actives. Carol

Osborne coordinated these activities. As part of this grant, MOFFA hosted a series of five regional roundtable discussions with certified organic farmers, and a one-half day workshop, "The Nuts and Bolts of Organic Farm Plans," for new and potential organic growers.

The Michigan Organic Conference

Building upon the success and popularity of the 1st Michigan Organic Conference (see above), the Michigan Organic Conference was held annually on the MSU campus from 2001 through 2011.

The Second Michigan Organic Conference in 2002 extended over three days and included workshops on a wide range of topics from Organic Vegetable and Flower Transplant Production to Dairy Processing to policy and marketing issues.

The conference in 2003 featured Percy Schmeiser, the third generation organic farmer from Saskatchewan who was sued by Monsanto for alleged violation of the patents on their GMO seed. His presentation was followed by a panel discussion with Chris Treter, Organic Consumers Association; Clare O'Leary with the Sierra Club, and Dr. Tom Zennie of OGM; moderated by Dr. Laura B. DeLind, MSU Sustainable Campus Initiative. The conference featured full day workshops on the first day and concurrent workshops on the second day organized into seven tracks: Soil Quality / Crop Ecology; Organic Certification; CSA / Marketing / Community Gardens; Food / Nutrition; Livestock / Field crops; Policies / Politics; and, a "Wild Card" session.

In 2005, the conference was entitled, "Growing Michigan's Organic Future". The keynote address was given by Maynard Kaufman on "Organic Farming and the Organic Way of Life."

John Biernbaum gave the keynote in the following year on "Honoring the Intentions of Organic" as well as a second presentation on "Building Successful Organic Farm Teams." There were ten education sessions that year, all but one focused on farming and the organic farmers. In 2006 there were also organic exhibitors, and the opportunity for regional organic team meetings.

The 2007 conference featured two keynote speakers: Jeff Moyer with the Rodale Institute and Elizabeth Henderson of Peacework Organic Farm, who addressed "A Just Harvest: Integrating Agroecology and Social Justice." The discussion sessions were organized into two tracks: morning discussions on Organic Production and afternoon sessions on Agricultural Marketing. There was also a consumer education session, "What's Really Organic?"

In 2008, the conference theme was "Bringing Consumers and Farmers Together!" Cheryl Rogowski, New York organic farmer and activist, gave the keynote address. There were almost 30 breakout sessions, including a session on How to be an Organic Activist. This conference also featured a Food System Film Festival as well as a session on Community Supported Agriculture in Michigan.

The 2009 conference, "Local Organic Food, Sustainable Prosperity for Michigan", featured Michael Sligh, Director of Just Food at the Rural Advancement Foundation International (RAFI-USA), who addressed the need for a "National Organic Action Plan", and Michael Phillips, nationally-known organic apple grower and author, who addressed the topic of "Circles of Connection: On the Farm, Embracing Community and Always in the Heart." Chris Bedford facilitated the first MOC Film Festival which featured five films during the conference. In addition to over 25 concurrent sessions, the conference included the reception "Taste of Michigan" and an "evening musical extravaganza" held at the Metrospace in East Lansing.

Over one dozen Michigan food producers and processors provided food for the conference.

The 2010 conference, "Michigan Organic: Seeds, Soil, and Health," was dedicated to the memory of Douglas Murray and Nancy Jones Keiser. Jeffrey Smith of the Institute for Responsible Technology gave the keynote address, "Don't Put That in Your Mouth: The Health Dangers of the Genetically Modified Foods You're Eating." He also gave an address on the second day, entitled, "Arming the Choir: How We Can Kick Out GMOs." There was also a Saturday afternoon address by C.R. Lawn of Fedco Seeds on "Growing Habitat: Embracing Biodiversity."

"Keeping the Local in Organic" was the theme of the conference in 2011. The keynote speaker was Mark Kastel of the Cornucopia Institute who spoke on "Protecting What We Have Built: The Agribusiness Takeover of the Organic Movement. Once again the conference featured a range of breakout sessions, followed by a "Taste of Michigan" social hour.

The 2011 conference was the last Michigan Organic Conference to be held at the Kellogg Center during ANR Week at MSU. The Michigan economy had sustained a relatively stunning blow with the recession of 2008, and recovery was slow. The support the conference had received from the Department of Agriculture, the MSU Extension, and MSU itself was no longer available. The MOFFA leadership had undergone virtually a complete turnover in the prior two years. With a board consisting of just six members in 2011, and with no paid staff, it was clear that MOFFA no longer had the resources to host a full conference.

An event in 2012 recognized the 20th anniversary of MOFFA and was oriented toward thinking about the future. The event was held in Flint in an effort to include urban farmers; the theme was "Bridging the Gap: Michigan Organic Celebration, Conversation and Collaboration."

After 2012, the MOFFA Board decided to focus on presentations at and sponsorship of the events of other related organizations, rather than hosting its own conference. This policy was followed through 2014.

MOFFA and the Michigan Food and Farming Community

The Mobile Food Processing Unit. In 1999, Susan Houghton, on behalf of MOFFA, received a USDA grant to create a mobile processing trailer designed to help state organic growers process their fruits and vegetables for the market. Several growers leased the trailer from MOFFA, but as early as 2001, the MOC carried an article titled, "MOFFA Trailer at Standstill?" In 2008, Fair Food Matters, non-profit group in Kalamazoo, was leasing the trailer, where it assisted in the development of the Can-Do Kitchen, a fully licensed kitchen which serves as an incubator for value-added food business startups. But the following year MOFFA once again solicited proposals for its use. In 2015 the trailer was donated to the Student Organic Farm at MSU.

Michigan Integrated Food and Farming Systems (MIFFS). MOFFA has always collaborated closely with MIFFS. Members participated in the MIFFS' USDA-funded Pilot Direct Marketing Project, and in 2001 MIFFS helped to produce several issues of *Michigan Organic Connections* before helping MOFFA acquire a new computer for that purpose. MOFFA is an annual supporter of the MIFFS Family Farms Conference.

Northern Michigan Small Farm Conference. MOFFA hosts an information booth every year at this one-day conference, and several MOFFA members typically present organic seminars as part of the program.

The Great Lakes Fruit and Vegetable Expo in Grand Rapids. Beginning in 2001, MOFFA has coordinated presentations on "Organic Day" at GLEXPO. MOFFA also typically hosts a booth at the event, and in some years has offered an evening reception. Participation in this annual event which draws thousands of farmers from around Michigan, other Great Lakes States, and Canada offers a way for MOFFA to reach conventional farmers to answer questions and provide information about organic production practices and organic certification.

Other Collaborative Activities. In October of 2001, MOFFA hosted a New Farmers Forum in Lawrence "to assist new and small-scale farmers, and to encourage dialog and networking opportunities." This was intended as a first meeting to encourage networking among state farmers. MOFFA member George Bird presented the keynote address, "Local Farms and Food Systems in the 21st Century."

Michigan Environmental Council. In 2002, MOFFA worked with the Michigan Environmental Council to review and raise public awareness of pesticides in the Great Lakes. MOFFA continues to be a member of the Council.

A Farmer's and an Eater's Pledge. In the Spring of 2007, the MOFFA Board reviewed the farmers pledge created by NOFA-New York (the Northeast Organic Farming Association of New York), and with NOFA's approval, adapted the pledge for Michigan Organic Farmers. In signing the pledge, farmers promise to: build and maintain healthy soils; protect the soil, water and air; use environmentally friendly farming methods; use traditional methods of plant and animal breeding; treat all livestock humanely; conserve the nutritional value of food; and use health and environment friendly processing methods. In addition, those signing the pledge agreed to: treat family members, volunteers and farm workers with respect, ensure their safety, and pay them as well as the situation permits; cooperate with other farmers to preserve farm land; cooperate with community leaders and members to create the most local food system possible; practice conservation of energy; support markets and infrastructures that enable small farmers to thrive; encourage biodiversity; and maintain the land in healthy condition for future generations of farmers.

Farmers also requested that MOFFA encourage consumers to pledge something back to the farmers. The idea of a Michigan Eater's pledge was to help consumers make a commitment to local organic and ecological food production. The thinking was that when farmers knew that they had the direct support of consumers, then they would be more likely to stay on the land and to continue their commitment to organic and ecological production methods.

The key features of the Eater's Pledge: spend at least 10% or $10 of the weekly food budget on locally grown and made organic foods (or those that carry the Michigan Farmers Pledge); buy food directly from local farms that are either certified or have signed the Farmers Pledge; choose local organic or Farmers Pledge foods when possible; learn to eat seasonally; encourage all food businesses to buy local organic and Farmer's Pledge products; try at least one new locally grown fruit or vegetable each week; preserve fresh seasonal foods; plan at least one meal each week featuring local organic or Farmer's Pledge food; and choose regionally grown, purchased and/or fair trade foods.

Surveying Michigan Organic Growers

In 2002, Jim Bingen worked with Susan Houghton on a Michigan Organic Growers Exploratory Survey. Bingen had recently completed a series of Crop & Pest Management Profiles with conventional growers, and after preliminary discussions with several members of OGM, worked with Susan to undertake 30 interviews with organic growers. The purposes of the interviews were: to test and design an interview survey; identify pest management practices used by organic growers; and, to compile and share the findings in order to discuss possible next program and policy steps. Some of the next steps included: identifying the kind of information that would be most useful to organic and "organic-transition" farmers; discussing the results with the Michigan Organic Advisory Committee; and preparing presentations for local communities to consider with respect to the contribution of organic agricultural practices to land use and to the revitalization of rural life in the state.

Drawing on the experience and the results of the exploratory survey, Bingen worked with Carol Osborne and Emily Reardon to complete the joint MSU-MOFFA 2006 Michigan Organic Survey. This survey was funded by two grants from the USDA. The survey was sent to over 250 certified operations in the state. Responses were received from 97 farmers and 19 processors (a 47% response rate).

The survey was modeled after the Biennial Surveys from the non-profit Organic Farming Research Foundation (OFRF) and included questions about: ownership, marketing in 2005; education; farm characteristics; regulatory and policy issues; and, processors: sources of products and marketing.

The report[1] of this first ever survey of organic growers and processors in Michigan included: the presentation of the survey results, insights from participants in roundtable discussions, marketing interviews with farmers, and interviews with fresh produce wholesalers and brokers. The results of this survey also contributed to the OFRF 3rd

---

[1] The survey report is available at http://moffa.net/f/MI_Organic _Agriculture_Report_March_2007.pdf.

National Survey of Organic Farming and to organic data compiled by the USDA/ERS.

Specific policy recommendations for Michigan included: a recommendation for a Biennial Census of Organic Agriculture in Michigan; the organization by MDA of an "organic summit" that recommended the creation of a Michigan organic identity; and research recommendations related to fertility management and to marketing issues and possibilities for collective marketing.

Efforts at Re-invigorating the Organic Movement in Michigan

In 2000, MOFFA considered ideas for "going local" by organizing regional "MOFFA groups" around the state. With the rapidly expanding use of, and access to the Internet MOFFA launched a website in 1996 and asked members to submit photos of farmhouses, barns, pastures, etc. to be used on the site.

By 2002, the publication *Eating Organically* was available in pdf format on the web. The publication was updated in 2003 and again in 2008. In 2013 the decision was made to limit the listings to growers, and a new name, *MOFFA's Guide to Michigan's Organic and Ecologically Sustainable Growers and Farms* reflected the change. For the first time the Farm Guide was primarily electronic, existing only online until 2015, when a paper copy was once again made available. In early 2017, the guide lists 145 farms, 97 of which are certified organic and the remainder have signed the Farmer's Pledge to assure customers that they are growing in an ecologically sustainable fashion,

From its earliest days, MOFFA's newsletter, *Michigan Organic Connections,* has served to keep members up to date on developments in organic agriculture, facilitate relationships among organic farmers and consumers, and stimulate thought and discussion on issues affecting the organic community. Beginning in 2011, the newsletter has been distributed primarily electronically, which has allowed us to reach many more people, while conserving precious funds to be used for other purposes (it is still printed and mailed to members who do not have email accounts). In 2014, a decision was made to focus each issue on a particular topic affecting organic agriculture, which has resulted in a series of substantial documents addressing the issues of our time. Readership continues to grow; in the spring of 2017 the mailing list contained over 1,390 names.

As the first decade of the 21st century drew to a close, and in light of the loss of Organic Growers of Michigan, there was a desire to (re)create a Michigan organic identity (and logo), and to increase the number of certified Michigan organic farmers.

The objectives of a proposed initiative in this area were to re-vitalize economic opportunities, strengthen the policy role of Michigan organic farmers, explore the issues raised by the state's organic farmers who decided to drop their organic certification in response to the changes wrought by the National Organic Program, and to identify options for creating a state policy voice for the Michigan organic community, with a goal of creating stronger markets for Michigan organic products and generating more consumer awareness of Michigan organic farmers, food and farming.

Based on the discussions around creating a "Michigan organic identity" as one step toward revitalizing the local and organic movement in Michigan, RAFI (Rural Advancement Foundation International—RAFI-USA) convened a National Organic Action Plan (NOAP) Summit[2] to begin work on several organic agriculture policy initiatives and "innovative marketplace goals." The idea of developing a "regional organic marketing infrastructure" that acknowl-

---

[2] The report arising out of this Summit is available online at http://rafiusa.org/docs/noap.pdf

edged and celebrated regionalism "by restoring local economies through support for local organic and fair foods infrastructure and labeling initiatives" was a central pillar of the RAFI idea.

For several members of MOFFA, this idea stimulated questions: how could we harness this idea to benefit both organic growers and consumers in Michigan and the region? As MOFFA moved into the second decade of the century, the combination of economic challenges, increasing familiarity with national certification, and the temporary loss of much of the MOFFA leadership in a short period of time caused the idea of a "Michigan organic identity" to recede. But the idea speaks to one of the cornerstones of MOFFA's mission: "to revitalize and sustain local communities."

MOFFA Leadership in the 21st Century

Of the founding members of the board, and those who joined them during MOFFA's first decade, only Maynard Kaufman and Pat Whetham remained on the board at the turn of the century.[3] Thirteen new members would join in the years 1999-2002; nearly half of those served less than two years. Of those who joined the board during this period, Carol Osborne, Nancy Jones Keiser, Jim Bingen, George Bird, and Doug Murray would go on to serve for most of the decade. Carol Osborne served as Chair for three years, from 2001 through 2003, and as Administrative Director 2004-2006; Jim Bingen was Chair 2005-2010.

As the century entered its second decade, the same pattern recurred. Of the nine members of the board at the beginning of 2010, none had been on the board for more than a year and a half, and most had served for less than a year. Jim Bingen had been forced to resign his position in

---

[3] A list of all of MOFFA's board members and officers appears as Appendix B, page 190.

2010 due to unexpected illness. Yvette Berman and Timothy Fischer shared the duties of Chair for that year, and in 2011 John Hooper was elected to the position, which he held through 2015 when personal considerations compelled him to resign. John Biernbaum was elected Chair in December, 2015 and continues to serve in that capacity in 2017.

The wholesale turnover around the year 2000 and again around 2010 affected MOFFA's course, as new board members with new priorities took over leadership of the organization. By 2012, the reduction in size of the board of directors, in combination with the lack of paid staff, meant that MOFFA no longer had the resources to present a yearly conference. Instead, it was decided that MOFFA would participate in and support the conferences of related

John Hooper with the MOFFA display, 2014

organizations, and John Hooper took on the task of display coordinator. His dedication to traveling to between six and ten events per year and setting up the MOFFA display and books available for sale makes it possible for this to remain a significant avenue of outreach for the organization.

A continuing thread throughout the history of both OGM and MOFFA has been the need for paid staff, and, through much of that time, the quest for funding to accomplish that state. Betty Edmunds served in a paid capacity from 1997 to 2001, and Carol Osborne was paid as Administrative Director from 2004 to 2006. After that time, there was no paid staff until 2012, when Kay Tremble was brought on as Administrative Assistant at ten hours per week. She resigned later that year and in January 2013 Julia Christianson took on the position.

In 2014, the organization's by-laws and articles of incorporation were amended to change the class of the organization from membership to directorship. MOFFA is still dependent on its members for financial support and direction, but it had become prohibitively difficult to gather a sufficient number of members in one place and time to have the quorum necessary to transact the business of the organization. With the change to a directorship basis, the board of directors is empowered to elect new directors and officers and make decisions to keep the organization running. The current by-laws still state that any member of the organization is eligible to run for election to the board of directors, and members are continually encouraged to volunteer and to communicate their opinions on the direction of the organization.

Organic Intensives

By the end of 2014, MOFFA's board included eleven members, and a "very part-time" Administrative Assistant had been secured. With more individuals involved, plans were made for a major event in 2015. The format chosen was a full-day intensive educational experience focused on one topic, on the model of the MOSES Organic University.

The first Organic Intensives was held on the MSU campus during ANR Week. Participants were offered a choice of three topics: Edible Landscaping and Permaculture Design, Cut Flowers for Profit and Diversification, or Compost, Vermicompost, and Compost Extracts and Teas. Over 100 people attended and the program was well received.

Organic Intensives was held again in 2016 and 2017, using the resources offered at MSU during ANR week. In 2016 the topics were Wild Edibles and Herbs, Organic Certification for Field Crop Farmers, and Seed Saving. The topics in 2017 were Organic Weed, Insect and Disease Management for the Diversified Vegetable Farm, Small Scale Success: Growing Nutrient Dense Vegetables in a Changing Climate, and The Changing Face of Field Crop Markets. In future years MOFFA would like to continue to offer educational opportunities in the Organic Intensives format in other areas of the state, and perhaps more than once a year.

MOFFA and National Policy Issues

Starting in the early 1990s, MOFFA's newsletter *Michigan Organic Connections* kept members up to date on a range of national food and farming issues. The most prominent issues included: the bovine growth hormone, RBGH; a range of food safety and pesticide use concerns including a review of the important book *Our Stolen Future;* and a discussion of the implications of the 1996 Food Quality Protection Act (FQPA), including a call for the disclosure of inert ingredients; and the use of arsenic-treated wood, especially for public playground equipment and for house decks. In addition to numerous and insightful reports on the national organic standards, issues related to the introduction and use of GMOs (genetically modified organisms or genetically-engineered (GE) crops) were of significant concern for several years.

MOFFA also used the *Michigan Organic Connections* newsletter to share reports from numerous national groups about concerns surrounding the use of crop biotechnology. For example, in 2000, the MOC carried a report from the Center for Food Safety on its Legal Challenge to Genetically Engineered Bt Crops. Perhaps most significant, in 2003, MOFFA hosted the Canadian grain farmer, Percy Schmeiser, who had launched an internationally-known legal challenge to Monsanto's highly restrictive seed-saving policies, to give the keynote address, "Biotechnology, Organic Farming and the Environment: Can we survive the GMO Generation?" to that year's organic conference.

In 2015, John Biernbaum was appointed to a 16-member NOP task force to explore hydroponic and aquaponic production practices and their alignment with USDA organic regulations. The discussion on this issue was contentious from the first, as approximately half the members of the task force represented traditional organic farming interests and the other half were representatives of large corporations which had invested heavily in hydroponic production,

John Biernbaum appeared before the National Organic Standards Board in the fall of 2016.

which in many cases had been certified organic for a number of years due to the inexact language of the "final rule" and inaction on NOSB's part to clarify the rule over the eight years since the issue first arose. The task force presented what was essentially two conflicting reports to the Standards Board in the fall of 2016.[4] The NOSB failed to make a decision on the issue at its meeting in the fall of 2016, and again at the spring meeting in 2017.

Looking Toward the Future

MOFFA's Annual Report[5] for 2016 suggests that the organization's activities will continue to focus primarily on education, and specifically on refining and expanding the Organic Intensives to multiple locations around the state, and possibly at multiple times of the year. Improving the content and usefulness of the newsletter is another priority, as is the development of a Vision Statement to carry the organization into the 2020s.

Dr. Jim Bingen is a Professor Emeritus, Community, Food and Agriculture in the Department of Community Sustainability at Michigan State University. He currently works on several applied research studies of organic farming and place-named foods and development in the Great Lakes States of the US, in Western Europe, and in French-speaking Africa. He was a Fulbright Distinguished Chair at the University of Natural Resources and Applied Life Sciences in Vienna, and he holds the Chevalier d'Ordre du Mérite Agricole, (Order of Agricultural Merit) awarded by the Government of France.

---

[4] Dr. Biernbaum reported on his experience on the task force in the September 2016 issue of Michigan Organic Connections: http://www.moffa.net/f/MichiganOrganicConnections-Sep2016.pdf.

[5] MOFFA's Annual Reports for the last several years are available on the website at http://www.moffa.net/annualreports.html.

PART III: Other Organic Groups and Activities

The Organic Movement at MSU

George W. Bird[1]

Michigan State University (MSU) was founded in 1855 by the Michigan Legislature as the Agricultural College of the State of Michigan. MSU is Michigan's Land Grant Institution under the Morrill Act of 1862, designed for specializing in "agriculture and the mechanical arts". In 1887, the U.S. Congress Hatch Act authorized establishment of the Michigan Agricultural Experiment Station (AES) and the Smith-Lever Act of 1914 resulted in the creation of the Michigan Cooperative Extension Service (CES). Under the leadership of President John Hannah (1941-1969), MSU became a *world-class* research institution, with a strong international focus. On a global basis, the Land Grant System of academic instruction, research and outreach (Extension) remains today, as the *envy of the world*!

This chapter provides a brief overview of the role of MSU in the Organic Movement in Michigan. It is presented as three eras: The Early Years (Pre-1990), The Reflective Years (1990-2000), and the National Organic Standards Era (2000 to 2017). Special reference is given to the MSU faculty, staff, and students involved in the development of organic agriculture in Michigan, our nation and internationally.

---

[1] *Bird, George W., Professor, Department of Entomology, Michigan State University, East Lansing, MI, 48842.*

The Early Years (Pre-1990)

Where to begin is a challenging question. Because of World War II, as a boy I spent a significant amount of time on a relative's poultry / dairy farm in southeastern Vermont. I clearly remember a morning in July of 1949, when one of my chores was to go with a tenant farmer boy to Chester Depot to meet a train that brought us a strain of earthworms that had been ordered from Rodale's *Organic Gardening* magazine. For the next three summers, I was responsible for feeding the refuse/residuals (not waste!!) from the *big house on the hill* (I did not live there) to the earth worms for production of compost for use as greenhouse potting soil.

Rachel Carson's *Silent Spring* (1962) caused me to reassess my academic sojourn in the synthetic chemotechnology side of conventional agriculture. Upon my arrival in 1973 as a faculty member at MSU, my colleagues (Herman Koenig, Dean Haynes, William Cooper, Lal Tumalla and Tom Edens) in the Departments of Entomology, Zoology and Electrical Engineering / System Science were in the process of designing something that became known as Integrated Pest Management (IPM). This was done in conjunction with faculty at the University of California-Berkeley, Cornell University, and Texas A&M. It is also noteworthy to indicate that Richard Harwood received his Ph.D. in Vegetable Breeding from the MSU Department of Horticulture during this time. In July of 1980, the first U.S. Organic Agriculture Report and Recommendations (the Bergland Report) was issued by the Carter Administration. Dick Harwood and Eliot Coleman were acknowledged by the Study Team. Under the leadership of Tom Edens (MSU Dept. of Resource Development), members of the Study Team visited with MSU faculty about the report. With the inauguration of President Reagan, the report was suppressed and members of the Study Committee fired. Among many comprehensive recommendations, the committee alluded to an *Organic Ethic*. This concept, however, was not included in the report.

In 1982, Patricia Michalik, an MSU undergraduate, indicated a desire to do a Master of Science thesis project on a comparative analysis of Collembola associated with conventional and organic production systems. It was known that the Rodale Institute had established a Long-Term Farming Systems Trial, with Dr. Richard Harwood as Director of Research. Patricia conducted her M.S. thesis research at the Institute and Dick (Dr. Harwood) served as a member of her MSU Graduate Committee. In the early 1980s, the MSU IPM Team played a major role in development of the concept of sustainable agriculture. This resulted in authorization of the Low Input Sustainable Agriculture (LISA) Program in the 1985 Farm Bill.

During the next five years, an increasing number of MSU faculty and students interacted with the Michigan organic community about the nature of organic agriculture. One area of agreement at this time was that soil forms the basis of organic systems. Unfortunately, MSU abolished its Department of Soil Science in the early 1960s. Joe Scrimger of Bio-Systems played the role of 'watchdog' and asked the hard questions about the relationships between MSU and conventional agriculture. John and Merrill Clark (Roseland Organic Farms) were also instrumental in the evaluation of MSU research / outreach and Michigan Department of Agriculture (MDA) policy in regard to organic agriculture. Between 1985 and 1990 small groups of experiment station researchers and extension service educators visited organic farms including the Robert Fogg Farm in Leslie, Michigan and the Richard Thompson Farm in Boone, Iowa. Both of these farms were part of the original Rodale Institute Network of Organic Farms. Dr. Laura DeLind of the MSU Department of Anthropology was a key leader in the Michigan organic movement at the time of the transition from the Early to Reflective Years.

The Reflective Years (1990-2000)

Three important events took place in 1990 in regard to the role of MSU in organic agriculture. These included the 1990 Farm Bill authorization and appropriations for the Sustainable Agriculture Research and Education Program (SARE), promulgation of the Organic Foods Production Act, and MSU hiring Dr. Richard Harwood as the first C.S. Mott Chair of Sustainable Agriculture. Between 1990 and 2000 there were lively debates within the academic community about the nature of organic agriculture. I had the distinct honor of being appointed as the first National Director of SARE (1991-1993). Final rules for the National Organic Program (NOP), however, were not published until 2000.

Funding for the C.S. Mott Chair was obtained under the leadership of the Chair of the MSU Department of Crop and Soil Science (Eldor Paul), and I served as chairperson of the Search and Recommendation Committee. It is alleged that after his appointment, Dr. Harwood was instructed by the administration to not use the *O-word* (organic) in regard to MSU programs. A finalist for the C.S. Mott Chair was a former Vice President of a well-known biotechnology corporation involved in developing genetically modified plant cultivars.

One of the most significant achievements during the Reflective Years was publication of *Michigan Field Crop Ecology* (1998) under the joint leadership of Dr. Harwood and Joe Scrimger. At a Sustainable Agriculture Education Session during the 1996 Agriculture and Natural Resources Week, growers were asked what type of educational materials would be most beneficial to them. They indicated that a farmer-friendly publication on field crop ecology, with special reference to how soil works, would be very helpful. A team of MSU faculty worked on this assignment for the next nine months. The manuscript was then reviewed by a team of farmers. Their verdict was presented at the 1997

Agricultural and Natural Resources Week. The evaluation clearly indicated that the MSU faculty had missed the mark and needed to go back to work taking the farmer recommendations into consideration. The grower-friendly *Michigan Field Crop Ecology* publication was released during the 1998 Agriculture and Natural Resources Week. It is now in its fifth edition and is one of the most successful initiatives I have been involved with. This initiative would not have been possible without involving the growers and other key members of the Michigan organic community. This is a key philosophy and policy of the SARE Program, which mandates growers as members of the Administrative Councils responsible for developing policy, allocating resources and assuring accountability through SARE Technical Review Committees, which also have farmer representation.

MOFFA (Michigan Organic Food and Farm Alliance) evolved from the Michigan Organic Growers Advancement Project (1992), and Dr. Laura DeLind served as a member of the Charter Board. She was also responsible for designing MOFFA's Local Food logo. MOFFA is the only organic advocacy organization in Michigan. An increasing number of MSU faculty provided articles for MOFFA's *Michigan Organic Connections*, formerly *Michigan Organic News*, in addition to participating in the Michigan Organic Harvest Festivals. Beginning in 1993, MOFFA sponsored what became the Michigan Organic Conference (formerly Organic Day) as part of the MSU Agriculture and Natural Resources Week. Under the leadership of Kathleen Merrigan (Administrator, USDA / AMS) the 2000 Federal Register codification and publication of the National Organic Program (NOP) changed the nature of the discussion, but not the tensions between the conventional and organic components of MSU faculty and students.

Organic Standards Era (2000 to 2017)

Publication of the final proposed rule for organic production in October of 2000 provided a long-needed framework for MSU faculty in regard to their organic agriculture initiatives. The 2001 Michigan Organic Conference included major MDA involvement in recognition of NOP. At this time, however, most telephone callers to County Extension Offices requesting information about organic agriculture were told that the information is not available and that organic agriculture is a *bad idea*.

By 2003, MSU claimed 17 organic agriculture research and outreach projects across 29 certified acres, 21 transitional acres, 2 acres managed organically and a 7-acre transitional student farm. These activities included contributions by the following 35 MSU participants: Paul Barrett, Bridget Behe, George Bird, John Biernbaum, Jim Bingen, Lisa Bohannen, Michael Cavigelli, Sean Clark, Andrew Corbin, John Davenport, Laura DeLind, Larry Dyer, Charles Edson, John Fisk, Stuart Gage, Larry Gut, Richard Harwood, Amy Irish-Brown, Bruce MacKellar, Tom Middleton, Dale Mutch, Ron Perry, Laura Probyn, Dan Rossman, Jose Sanchez, Annemeik Schilder, Phil Schwallier, Mike Score, Joe Simmons, Susan Smalley, George Sundin, Kurt Thelen, Gary Thorton, Mark Whalon and Tom Zabadal.

The *2001-2003 State of the States: Organic Farming Research at Land Grant Institutions* published by the Organic Farming Research Foundation praised MSU for its individual projects and faculty, but was negative in regard to the fact that MSU did not have a coordinated Organic Agriculture Program. Following this initial surge, a number of MSU faculty and CES educators emerged as true innovators and leaders within the Michigan organic community. These included John Biernbaum, Matt Grieshop, Dan Rossman, Jim Bingen and Vicki Morrone. Following the retirement of Dr. Harwood in 2002, Dr. Michael Hamm became the C.S. Mott Chair of Sustainable Agriculture.

Jim Bingen retired in 2013 as Professor Emeritus in the MSU Department of Community Food and Agriculture. In addition to playing major leadership roles on the Board of MOFFA, Carol Osborne, Emily Reardon and Jim published a comprehensive *Survey of Michigan Organic Agriculture*. They reported that in 2005, Michigan had 225 certified organic farms, comprising 45,500 acres or 0.4% of Michigan crop land. Michigan ranked in the top 20 states in regard to certified organic acreage. It ranked first in regard to organic spelt, second for organic beans, and sixth for organic fruit. Jim is a past president of the Agriculture, Food and Human Values Society. In addition, he is a recipient of the *Chevalier d'Ordre du Mérite Agricole* (National French Order of Agricultural Merit) award and a Fulbright Distinguished Chair at the University of Natural Resources and Applied Life Sciences in Vienna.

Dr. John Biernbaum is a true organic scholar. His courses in the Department of Horticulture include *Organic Farming Principles and Practices, Compost Production and Use, Organic Transplant Production,* and *Passive Solar Greenhouses for Protected Cultivation.* John conducts compost research, with special reference to vermiculture. He is nationally recognized for his knowledge and innovations about organic season extension through the use of solar-based hoop-houses, and is continually in demand as a presenter at major conferences such as MOSES (Midwest Organic and Sustainable Education Service) and NMSFC (Northern Michigan Small Farm Conference). Dr. Biernbaum was the key faculty member interacting with MSU undergraduate students in the development of MSU's Student Organic Farm. This 15-acre certified organic farm has operated on a 48-week per year cycle, providing field and hoop-house produce to its CSA (Community Supported Agriculture) members and seven months of sales to MSU dining halls, wholesale outlets, and a campus-based farm stand. Under John's direction, the farm provided a highly innovative eight-month Organic Farmer Training Program, serving students of very diverse backgrounds and ages. Dr. Lauri Thorp successfully introduced both poultry and hogs into the system; the Farm Manager (Jeremy Moghtader) recently departed to become the University of Michigan Campus Farm Manager. The fall harvest season is celebrated with the Hoop House Gala, sponsored by Vinnie Gore (MSU VP for Culinary Services). The event is designed to generate scholarships for students enrolled in the Organic Farmer Training Program.

In 2006, the MSU Provost granted the Department of Entomology a position in Organic Pest Management. Dr. Matt Grieshop was the successful candidate. This is the first of only two faculty position at MSU with the word "Organic" in the position title. Matt's program focuses on organic agriculture, biological control of insects, insect behavior, agroecology, and integrated pest management. He provided leadership for the integration of livestock into apple production systems in the upper Midwest. The science of this initiative has been significantly enhanced through the dedication of Dr. Dale Rozeboom of the MSU Department of Animal Science. Matt has also been successful in the development of on-site biological control agent rearing protocols for Michigan greenhouse pest control. Most of Matt's research is on-farm with major farmer participation. He has been responsible for organizing the annual organic fruit session at GLEXPO (Great Lakes Expo in Grand Rapids). Matt also provides administrative leadership for the MSU Clarkesville Research Station.

The Center for Regional Food Systems was developed in the MSU Department of Community Sustainability under the leadership of Dr. Michael Hamm (C.S. Mott Chair of Sustainable Agriculture). As part of this program, Vicki Morrone serves as the Organic Farming Outreach

Specialist for field and vegetable crops. A very dynamic individual, she is responsible for the annual Michigan Organic Reporting Session and the Organic Day at GLEXPO. Interacting with Professor Sieglinde Snapp, Vicki specializes in soil building and has been involved in farmer-focused programs throughout the U.S. and Africa.

Although MSU still does not have a centrally coordinated organic agriculture program, former students and current organic farmers such as Jessie and Leah Smith (Nodding Thistle Farm) are contributing in a highly positive manner with their articles about Michigan organic agriculture. The 2017 MSU Extension website lists ten organic educational programs, each under the leadership of a different individual (Charles Gould, George Silva, Ben Phillips, Rufus Isaacs, Eric Hanson, Bob Battel, Jerry Lindquist, Brad Baughman, Collin Thompson and Jim Isleib). Because of population collapse in a number of Michigan cities such as Detroit (1.8 million population in 1950 and 640,000 in 2017), there is a significant amount of vacant urban land. Some of this is being successfully used for certified organic crop production. In 2016, MSU earmarked $300,000 to establish a Center for Urban Food Systems in Detroit.

In 2017, MSU has a variety of organic initiatives that are well-coordinated with the organic community, and the MSU Student Organic Farm is undergoing a significant reorganization. MSU also provides information derived from secondary sources without meaningful interactions with organic growers, processors or marketers. For the faculty who have had direct, meaningful interactions with the organic community, the experiences have been highly rewarding.

Since this chapter began with one of my life stories, it is appropriate to conclude it in a similar manner. As an MSU faculty member I have learned much from the organic community. One example is the process described in "Climbing Mt. Organic: An Ecosystem Approach to Pest Management" written jointly by Paul Hepperly, Jeff Moyer, Matt Grieshop and myself.[2] Another member of the organic community that I have worked with extensively is Fred Kirschenmann of Kirschenmann Family Farms (Biodynamic) of North Dakota and the Leopold Center (Iowa State University). In our 2006 contribution entitled "A Question of Ethics and Productivity",[3] Fred and I presented the following Organic Ethic (based on Mahatma Gandhi's Seven Deadly Social Sins); something that was missing in the Bergland Report:

Farming systems must:
- *be regenerative in nature,*
- *be cooperating partnerships with ecological interdependence,*
- *be based on family enterprises designed to maintain vibrant communities that generate intergenerational equity,*
- *generate appropriate wealth through work and*
- *foster commerce inoculated with morality and politics with principles.*

In addition, we recognized organic agriculture as an essential component of global food security that:

> *must restore the ecological health of the natural resources upon which agriculture depends, while climate is changing, when global society insists that food is a human right, when infectious diseases*

---

[2] Bird, G., M. Grieshop, P. Hepperly and J. Moyer. 2009. "Climbing Mt. Organic: An Ecosystem Approach to Pest Management". In *Organic Farming: The Ecological System*, C. Francis (ed). Soil Science Society of America, IA.

[3] Kirschenmann, F. and G. Bird. 2006. "A Question of Ethics and Productivity". In *Developing and Extending Sustainable Agriculture: A New Social Contract*, C. Francis, R. Poincelot and G. Bird (eds). Haworth Press, NY.

require that we attend to ecological ramifications of human activities and when farmers must retain a sufficient share of the value of their productivity to be economically viable.

At the 2016 GLEXPO Trade Show, the words *Organic, Sustainability,* and *Soil Health* were commonly displayed. It must never be forgotten that Healthy Soil forms the basis of organic agriculture. Since 2011, the Michigan potato industry has provided extensive leadership for development of a true understanding of the nature of soil health. While many socio-economic challenges exist, it appears that members of the conventional agricultural community are beginning to listen to the organic agriculture community and vice versa. While this should be considered a positive development, as a nematologist I will conclude by saying,

LISTEN TO THE WORMS.

George W. Bird is a Professor in the Department of Entomology at Michigan State University and former Research Scientist, Agriculture Canada and Associate Professor, University of Georgia. He received his B.S. and M.S. from Rutgers University and the Ph.D. at Cornell University. George spent much of his childhood on a poultry/dairy farm in southeastern Vermont, and managed an apple orchard in western Massachusetts during his high school years. He has been at MSU since 1973, where he teaches, does research on soil-borne issues, and works closely with both organic and conventional growers. In addition, Dr. Bird served as the first National Director of the U.S. Sustainable Agriculture Research and Education Program.

The Student Organic Farm at MSU

John Biernbaum

Previous publications regarding the Student Organic Farm (SOF) have come from the perspective of evaluating either the teaching programs and our work with students (Biernbaum et al. 2006; Biernbaum, 2011) or the production systems used (Biernbaum, 2008b). The lens here is to focus on the historical development of the SOF in the context of the growth of Michigan organic agriculture. It is an honor to have the Michigan State University SOF included as part of the Organic Movement in Michigan. The early stages of development of the SOF were very catalyzing and eventually transformative for all involved. The development of the SOF also influenced the perception of many MSU staff, faculty and administrators regarding organic farming.

Development

The SOF grew out of a meeting of about 18 students, staff and faculty held in April 1999 (Biernbaum, 2008b). The graduate and undergraduate students were primarily members of a registered student organization called the Michigan Sustainable Agriculture Network that was formed in 1994 with the support of the first C.S. Mott Endowed Chair for Sustainable Agriculture, Dr. Richard Harwood, and Extension Specialist Susan Smalley. During the fall semester of 1999 and spring 2000 there were several meetings to discuss a variety of ideas about how a teaching farm could develop. In spring semester 2001 we convened a selected topics class on "What is Organic?" with a goal of moving forward the idea of a teaching farm. There were about ten students who worked together to develop a shared vision for an organic teaching farm.

In early 2001 a research proposal to study organic production of winter salad greens in high tunnels was submitted and eventually funded by USDA special funding for Sustainable Agriculture at MSU under the direction of Dick Harwood. In January I attended a winter farming conference in Albany, New York and in February visited Eliot Coleman at his farm. In August the first two high tunnels were constructed at the Horticulture Teaching and Research Center (HTRC) research site that eventually became the SOF.

Fall semester 2001 a new registered student organization known as the Student Organic Farm Initiative (SOFI) was started by about ten students. Several of these students attended the first Kellogg Food and Society Conference held in Pittsburg. We worked on writing the foundation of what became funding proposals submitted to the W.K. Kellogg Foundation and the USDA Higher Education Challenge Grant in 2002. The Kellogg grant of $95,000 was received in the summer of 2002 but the $100,000 USDA grant had to be submitted a second time before being funded in 2003.

Part of the process of creating the SOF involved visiting organic farms and other student farm programs. Several students completed internships on organic farms in Michigan, like Growing in Place CSA in Mason, and around the country. Most of those same students became the first SOF employees in 2003.

Also relevant to the development of the SOF was the report *Cultivating Organic Agriculture in Michigan* published by the Michigan Organic Advisory Committee in 1999. One of the committee's recommendations was for MSU to provide organic farming related teaching programs and research. This report provided the justification within

MSU for the SOF and later for the Organic Farmer Training Program.

Based on observation of SOF-like programs at other universities, our original perception was that we needed to be on the main campus or very close to campus where we could be visible and accessible. On the other hand, being out on the HTRC at the southern edge of campus was likely an advantage that kept us below the University radar in the early years. The HTRC staff and the Horticulture Department financial staff were very supportive and essential to the success of the SOF.

During the fall of 2002, three more high tunnels were built to form the nucleus of the SOF. Students worked every Saturday for ten weeks in what remains the highlight of my time at MSU. The students were so passionate and motivated to finally be starting the farm that had been talked about for several years. I had read about the early days (1855-1875) of MSU when students and faculty worked side by side in the fields for part of the day. This connection is so important compared to classroom time. It is what our students really want but rarely get.

Another class of about ten students during the spring 2003 semester developed the detailed implementation plans for the year-round 48-week CSA. The first SOF farm manager, Michelle Ferrarese, started as a graduate student at MSU in January 2003 and guided the first high tunnel plantings in February and the first CSA distribution in May. About 1.5 acres of field vegetables including plenty of storage potatoes, onions, winter squash and cabbage completed the mix for the 25 CSA memberships.

Some important farmers and Organic Growers of Michigan (OGM) members who supported early development of the SOF included Susan Houghton from Giving Tree Farm, Pat Whetham, and Jayne Leatherman-Walker. Joe Scrimger came to the farm for one of our first hoophouse tours and over the years that followed provided me some important and much appreciated advice and understanding of organic farming.

Important influences we were fortunate to have within MSU were Dick Harwood, Susan Smalley, George Bird, Jim Bingen and Laura DeLind. The collegial sharing of information and ideas was so important. I like to give Laura DeLind the credit she deserves for the influence she had on my perceptions of community farming through the chance to see and experience Growing in Place CSA in Mason. She also recommended two important books to me that provided the vision of what we needed to do. *Reclaiming the Commons* by Brian Donahue and *Farms of Tomorrow Revisited* by Trager Groh and Steven McFadden provided the images of CSA and farm land held in public trust to allow easier transfer to the next farmer. Being able to see what is possible is so important to a growing movement. The proposal made by Brian Donahue in *Reclaiming the Commons* that every community should have a school, an athletic field and a diversified year-round community teaching farm is still a part of my mission in this life.

In 2004 the SOF Organic Systems Plan was submitted to Organic Growers of Michigan, as the first step in the process of achieving organic certification. The first inspection completed by Nancy Jones Keiser is another historical highlight. That process and how our team of student organic farmers all learned from Nancy is what I share as part of the story of what inspections were and what they have become. The arrival of the first certificate that fall was a movement milestone and cause for celebration.

During the 2004 annual MOFFA fall celebration I was surprised to be presented with the MOFFA Public Service Award. I still find myself sharing the importance of how in those early years, when I knew little of organic farming and the bigger picture of the importance of our food systems, how supportive and tolerant people were. The friendly sharing of ideas is a key characteristic of the organic farming movement.

Part of the forming of the SOF was an attempt to cultivate a program that integrated teaching, research, outreach and service. My personal experience of these four pillars of the Land Grant philosophy and mission was that there was more separation than integration. We later also tried to integrate "academics" with university "operations" by providing food for consumption on campus. In both cases there appeared to be verbal administrative support, but few if any signs of real support for the work that integration requires. Having undergraduate students and CSA members routinely at the Horticulture Teaching and Research Center was something outside the norm that took a while to be accepted and embraced. The need to connect students to daily agricultural practice continues to grow.

> Guiding The SOF —
>
> Farmers, friends and families using facts and feelings to physically, faithfully and fearlessly farm front yards, forests and fields for food, feed, fodder, forage, fiber, fuel, flowers, fertility, fun, freedom, fairness and the future.
>
> — John Biernbaum

The SOF also needed to be a place where diverse ideas were welcomed. Students from a wide range of MSU classes came to the SOF for tours and experienced the organic movement. Graduate student Emily Reardon was the tour organizer as well as assistant farm manager. In many cases students were able to talk with fellow students and share the experience first-hand. We shared the story of the living soil and the soil food web, showed how we were composting and using compost to build soil, shared the high tunnels and cold storage methods for season extension, and introduced the concept of CSA programs for marketing for local food when most visiting the farm had never heard of Community Supported Agriculture.

In the early years of the SOF development, it was the students—among them Lynn Rhodes, Seth Murray, Bev Ruesink, Adam Montri, Anna Bosma, Jessica Long, Joe Redmond, Michael Rodriquez, Fred Monroe, Trevor Johnson, Ben Gluck, Solomon Jost, Andy Fogiel, Michelle Ferrarese, Emily Reardon, and others—who made the difference and provided the 'move' in movement. There is something powerful about students becoming teachers for their fellow students. We eventually moved to full time staff positions to provide continuity of management in the program. In hindsight, while the SOF gained stability and perhaps sustainability with full time staff, there was a loss of the energy and enthusiasm of motivated students that was so critical to developing the initial momentum.

Teaching and Outreach Programs

The SOF gradually grew to four acres of production, 50 CSA memberships, and a stable production and rotation plan in 2005. My perception is that while we wanted to teach about organic farming from the very beginning, it was important for us to first get some experience with organic farming. The first plans for a formal classroom and on-farm teaching program started in 2005. After much work on curriculum and course development and approval, the first group of students in the Institute of Agriculture Technology 11-month Organic Farming Certificate Program started in January 2007. The program continued as an Ag Tech certificate for three years prior to shifting to a nine-month non-credit outreach program in 2010 through 2016. On average there were 14 to 16 participants per year. A strength of the program was the immersion in day to day crop production and operation of the farm, CSA program and Farm Stand.

Development of the teaching program was supported by three years of funding from MSU (at $30,000 per year) as well as $75,000 grant support. *Partnering to Cultivate Organic Agriculture in Michigan and the Midwest* was a $750,000, three-year (2006-2008) grant from the USDA Organic Research and Education Program that supported objectives related to field crops, vegetables, marketing and education. Faculty members involved included Sieg Snapp, Dale Mutch, Jim Bingen, George Bird, John Biernbaum, Mathieu Ngouajio, and Mike Brewer. The funding allowed us to add Corie Pierce to the team as coordinator for the certificate program.

Starting in 2004, partnerships with Michigan Food and Farming Systems (MIFFS) under the guidance of Elaine Brown, the USDA Natural Resources Conservation Service (NRCS), and the USDA Risk Management Agency Community Partnership Program (2006-2010) were all key to developing outreach programs for the SOF. A focus on minority and limited resource farmers led to important projects and connections in Detroit with Greening of Detroit and later Keep Growing Detroit, and in Flint with Edible Flint. This funding supported adding Adam Montri to the SOF team to provide hoophouse outreach.

The basic concepts of reducing risk were the organic farming principles learned from visiting organic farms:

1. Build Soil Organic Matter
2. Increase Crop, Livestock and General Farm Biodiversity
3. Use Season Extension and Year-round Farming
4. Develop Direct and Diverse Markets

These SOF programs were able to reach several audiences interested in organic farming. This was really the growing of the movement from a core to an extended family and community.

- From 10 to 15 students a year were at the farm as employees or volunteers on a regular basis. Many of these students started farming or working with food related careers after leaving the SOF.
- Each year hundreds of MSU students and Lansing Community College students come to the farm for an hour or two to hear about organic farming and local food.
- On average 10 to 15 participants of the Organic Farmer Certificate (11-month Ag Tech) or Organic Farmer Training Program (9-month non-credit) courses were at the farm for intensive training.
- The Organic Farming Principles and Practices course offered by the Horticulture Department starting in 2007 brought 20 to 30 students per year to the farm.
- Minority and limited resource farmers initially with MIFFS (2004-2006) and later with the USDA Risk Management Agency Community Farming program (2006 to 2010) visited the farm.
- Farmers and gardeners participating in workshop and extension programs either visited the farm or attended presentations around the state about the SOF and Organic Farming.

The rapid growth in certified organic land in Michigan during the 1990s and 2000s was primarily due to growth in bean and grain crops produced in the thumb region. But the number of new CSA vegetable farmers using organic methods and season extension was also growing.

The SOF was a catalyst for season extension as much as organic farming. The combination of small scale with year-round intensive vegetable and fruit production has provided new opportunities for many beginning farmers of all ages—younger farmers and second career farmers. When first learning about CSA as a method of providing local vegetables for 20 to 24 weeks, the question that came to mind was "What happens during the other half of the year?" Coming from a greenhouse management background, I was used to growing year-round. I had also been introduced to Eliot Coleman and four season farming and cold storage methods at a farmer's conference in Albany New York in February 2001. I hope that the 48 week CSA will be seen as a contribution of the SOF to the organic movement in Michigan. Farming year-round provides opportunities for seasonal stability and employment. But farming year-round is not for everyone and comes with challenges and infrastructure needs.

Starting in 2014, following a review and renaming of the Upper Peninsula Research and Education Center (UPREC) in Chatham Michigan, a new outreach, research and teaching farm was started. The North Farm under the direction of Matt Raven in the Department of Community Sustainability, Station Director Ashley McFarlan, and farm manager Collin Thompson is providing an incubator farm modeled in part after the SOF. The farm was certified organic in 2016 and is providing another point in MSU AgBioResearch and MSU Extension for multiple audiences to experience organic agriculture. A CSA Farm has also been established at the Novi Tollgate Center in Oakland County.

Closing Reflection

To me organic farming always just made sense. It wasn't a revolt or revolution, it was practical use of available and natural resources. Why pay for something that is available for free or locally available with some physical effort? I like how Eliot Coleman tells the story of how the USDA said that organic fertilizers were no different than industrial / processed fertilizers. Rather than consider that a put-down, Eliot considered it confirmation that there was nothing wrong with organic farming.

My hope in sharing the SOF story as part of the Organic Movement in Michigan is that others will remember how the passion of a few people with a shared vision can proliferate and promote a common purpose. The addition of financial support can increase the rate at which an organization is able to grow. But growth that is limited by the challenges of scavenging and being efficient by necessity is likely to be more sustainable than unrestricted growth achieved with excessive inputs.

A focus of my personal reading prior to and during the development of the SOF and learning about organic farming was on the nature of personal and social change. Movements are the outcome of both individuals and communities. There is the personal struggle of dark nights or time in the desert leading up to the transition and enlightenment. And there is the work of sharing and being with others. As I write this, I am reminded of the effort to share what I had been learning about personal growth in the keynote presented at the 2006 Michigan Organic Conference (Biernbaum, 2006).

"What is Organic Farming?", "Why Organic Farming?", and "How to Farm Organically?" continue to be important and common questions. The SOF, and now the North Farm, continues to be a place where people can come and find answers through first-hand experience.

I recently read a proposal that keeping marijuana illegal and viewed as a dangerous thing and associating it with the counterculture was likely part of a strategy to marginalize a group of people who did not accept the political premise that industrialization and urbanization were essential for economic and societal development. One can also consider that minimizing and disparaging organic farming was a similar conscious effort with the same intended outcome. Time will test the impacts of excessive industrialization and urbanization. In the meantime, cultivating the space for alternative visions and ideas is an opportunity for each of us to be a part of our organic farming past, present and future.

That said, I have had to write this from the perspective of being disassociated from the management of the SOF since early 2015, when I was told by administrators of the College of Agriculture and Natural Resources (CANR) that I could no longer be involved in the SOF. Trying to explain what happened would only be speculation on my part. A management structure was put in place that involved no direct faculty oversight, with the farm manager reporting to an administrator and advisory committee with little knowledge of farming or organic farming. In 2016 the future of the management and organization of the SOF is in question. Despite the recognition of efforts of MSU students and faculty relative to the SOF, the North Farm, and other organic projects, it may be that the organic movement and its rejection of genetic engineering (GMOs) may still be seen as a threat, to be smiled at and kept at a distance.

I do not know what the SOF will be or do in the future, but my wish is that it can continue to grow with the help of students working to keep the 'Student' in Student Organic Farm. The SOF and the North Farm can be models of diversified organic year-round farms that contribute to a growing organic movement, with the goal of cultivating within all of us the best of being human.

References

Biernbaum, J. 2011. "Four Season Farming and Learning". In Fields of Learning: The Student Farm Movement in North America. Ed. Laura Sayre and Sean Clark. University Press of Kentucky.

Biernbaum, J. 2006. The Marriage of Sense and Soul: Developing Integral Agriculture. Available at: http://www.hrt.msu.edu/people/dr_john_biernbaum. 15 pgs

Biernbaum, J. 2008a. MSU Student Organic Farm Strategic Plan. Available at: http://www.hrt.msu.edu/people/dr_john_biernbaum. 98 pgs

Biernbaum, J. 2008b. "Year-round Food and Learning at MSU". The Natural Farmer. Fall 2008, pgs 14-19. Available at: http://www.nofa.org/tnf/Fall2008.pdf.

Biernbaum, J.A., Thorp, L. and Ngouajio, M. 2006. "Development of a Year-round Student Organic Farm and Organic Farming Curriculum at Michigan State University". HortTechnology 16(3):20-24.

Donahue, B. 1999. Reclaiming the Commons: Community Farms and Forests in a New England Town. Yale University Press. 349 pgs.

Groh, T. and S. McFadden. 1977. Farms of Tomorrow Revisited, Community Supported Farms Farm Supported Communities. Biodynamic Farming and Gardening Association, Kimberton, PA. 294 pgs.

Student Organic Farm Website: http://www.msuorganicfarm.org.

John Biernbaum holds degrees in Horticultural Science from North Carolina State University (B.S.), Pennsylvania State University (M.S.), and Michigan State University (Ph.D.). He joined the MSU faculty in the Horticulture Department in 1985. His primary responsibility is teaching several courses including Organic Farming Principles and Practices, High Tunnels, Organic Transplants, and Compost Production and Use. In recent years his research has focused on composting campus food residues, with a special interest in vermicomposting. He routinely provides outreach presentations supporting small-scale year–round diversified organic agriculture including urban agriculture. He has been a member of the board of directors of Michigan Organic Food and Farm Alliance since 2009, and presently serves as the organization's Chair.

Organic Farmers of Michigan

An Interview with Dean Berden

Maynard Kaufman: Thank you for letting us interview you. Don't hesitate to add details in addition to answering the following questions.

Dean Berden: OK.

MK: OK. We understand from the website of Organic Farmers of Michigan that you were one of 19 farmers who started the organization in 1990 and that you are still one of the officers, the Secretary.

DB: That's so.

MK: Our first question, when and why did you originally decide to go organic?

DB: Well, that's a couple of questions. First I'll talk about how OFM started. I got together with Ernie Fordos. At that time, I would have been about 40 years old, and he was in his 70s, he was like a father figure to me. Anyway, he saw that we needed to have some type of organization—he was getting totally different prices than we were. He and I talked back and forth; we got a group of guys together in my area, in the Thumb, and his area, west of Saginaw. We all agreed to get together at the restaurant in Owasso—I'd need to look up the date. We were all shocked at how much pricing difference these brokers and buyers were offering us.

To go on to the next subject, you asked how I got started. As a really small child, I loved to pitch in and work with my grandfather and dad, and I loved to fill my pockets full of earthworms. When I started farming, I got into chemical farming—that was the trend at the time, in the '60s, '70s—I noticed as were doing that, that less and less earthworms were in our soil all the time. And that's one of the indicators of soil health, plant health too, for corn and soybeans and so on. We were doing the wrong thing—all these chemicals were poisoning the soil. So I started playing with different ideas, without putting on chemical fertilizers and pesticides.

In the early 80s, playing around with it, I joined Organic Growers of Michigan and was a member of that for several years. Trying to develop markets, we decided the only way to do it was to go to some of these natural foods shows. The first year I grew my first organic navy beans, I ended up selling them locally, didn't get anything for them. My wife and I went to all kinds of different areas and did all we could to find a market. Then we found Eden Foods— they were the first ones we sold a lot of beans to. We've got a processing plant now, and we still sell a lot of beans to them.

MK: Have you been on the board of directors of OFM regularly ever since you started in 1990?

DB: At that time I was teaching school; I was the only one to write on the blackboard, so they said, "you're it." When I started putting commodities up there, all these different types of beans, and now "I got this price," and somebody else said, "I got this price," we all agreed to put in— everybody put in $25 for mailing and information. We got together the next year and started talking about putting in $1 an acre, so for 200 acres, $200, to spread the benefit if we get the higher prices. That worked for a few years, and more complex systems developed from there.

MK: How many members do you have right now?

DB: About 56 members, but we're marketing for over 100 farmers.

MK: Are you organized as a co-op or—what's your legal status?

DB: LLC. We did a bunch of research with a lawyer. There's the Capper-Volstead Act that puts restrictions on setting prices. So what we did is we researched it, and there's nothing to stop us from coming up with what we called target prices—something we wanted to achieve, or had already received. Over 8 of the last—well, 26 years now—over the last probably 15 of those years we have published in the Acres paper, and we also have an ad now in the non-GMO paper; we put in advertising with target

Organic Farmers of Michigan Field Day, August, 2015

prices. Buyers aren't happy with that, but we never have been sued yet. We publish so that new farmers that come in—we're trying to give people a benchmark for what you should be receiving, in this area.

MK: Are all of your members in the Thumb area?

DB: No, we have members in Ohio, Indiana, Wisconsin, and all over Michigan. And there are some farmers who market through us but aren't members.

MK: What do you do for your members?

DB: Mainly we provide a marketing service. We have a full time marketing person and a full time office person. We market all types of commodities.

MK: How much better are your prices than conventional?

DB: Typically double, sometimes triple. But I don't call it conventional, I call it chemical.

MK: How much of the produce that you sell is exported, and how much is sold in this country?

DB: I used to know all those things ... it used to be over 50% went to foreign markets, now it's probably 10% because there's such a developing market in this country. My wife is really involved in politics, she talks to a lot of politicians and their spouses, and a lot of the time they're eating organic too.

A lot of people in the cities understand about GMO. They have a pretty good idea what GMOs are, and what the ramifications are. I was talking to a neighbor the other day, a young fellow, and he got really insulted when I said, "you've got a real problem on your hands." All the sugar beets now in Michigan are GMO—well, I could talk an hour on that but—I was just saying you have a problem, you've got a perception in the general populace that GMO is bad.

We do ship some to Japan, some to England, some to Italy, but like I said, less than before. Less by far.

MK: Is Herbruck's a major customer?

DB: They buy a lot of corn from us in this area, yes.

MK: Are beans the largest export?

DB: Export out of this country, yes, but corn is probably the highest acreage, high value too. But we do a lot of dry beans; 99% of our business is food grade beans—soybeans and adzuki beans, when I first started organically, and started with Eden. Most of those sales now are domestic because we have a lot of Asian people here in this country now. In 1999 my wife and I went to Japan, a food show there, but the dollar is so high now, the value difference— that's another political thing.

MK: The spring issue of your newsletter reported there is pressure to lower prices for organic field crops.

DB: Not necessarily exports, but all crops. Prices for chemical crops have lowered drastically. A few years ago farmers were getting $7 to $8 for corn on the chemical market, and $12 to $13 for organic. Now chemical is down 50%, to $3 to $4, and we're talking $8 to $9 for organic. So there is some pressure to lower it. We've got some farmers who think for themselves only, but we've got to stick together. Prices on imported beans are also affecting product now.

MK: I remember that Richard Harwood once said that your soils had the highest levels of organic matter of any in the state. How did you achieve that?

DB: Well, he called me up, asked if I was willing to let him take a soil test. I said yeah, we can do that, so he had some grad students do it. Then he came back and said, I think we made a mistake, we need to resample, and can I bring some of my professor friends and grad students. I said as long as you don't take all day, but a couple hours we can deal with it. The field was at my home.

When the van from MSU came, a little fellow jumps out of the van. He said, "We don't know what you think you're doing, but you can't do what—" ...then Richard got out and apologized. OK. So I showed them some of the fields. They looked at one field in particular, a field quite a bit lower than the road, and this little fellow was walking around this soybean field, looking across the road at a chemical field, which was sparser by far than my field. So we got back after a two hour tour and the little professor says, OK, you did it, but just how do you do it? I said, "I don't know, you're the smart guy, you figure it out." We've learned, with compost, green manures, to not burn our soil, not to sunburn it—we've learned a lot of things.

We were certified first in 1986 and 1987 with OGM, then we switched to OCIA and were internationally certified in 1988, that's when we started selling soybeans to Japan. In 1986 we stated doing a little processing, because nobody else was doing it. The first thing you know, I had 25 or 30 customers, and we built up a plant.

MK: So how high was the organic matter in your soil?

DB: It was in the normal range in our area, two and a half to three percent. Most of it in our area now is five to six percent. The chemical folks plow in the fall and leave it bare all winter. If you left your skin outside unprotected it would dry out and crack, same with the soil. It can get sunburned the same as people. That's how we were doing it, doing it for years. We're working with it now to try to bring it back.

MK: You did this all with green manures?

DB: Green manures, composts, all kinds of things. Residue, leave it all on the surface. Right now we're getting an oat cover crop out in the spring, not for harvest, but just for a cover crop. We'll let it grow to four, five, six inches, then work it in good. There's some allelopathy there, it really bumps up on weed control. I had an article in Rodale Press about green manures. When we do our weeds, we put in red clover. My great grandfather used clover seed, and alfalfa. It's all about production, putting residue back into the soil, developing the nitrogen fixing material to help us produce good quality crops naturally.

MK: Thanks so much, we appreciate your answers to our questions. Do you have anything to add?

DB: About Organic Farmers of Michigan, we had a couple of different marketers we went through. Some of them jumped and formed their own groups, which fell apart a few years later. There have been quite a few groups around the U.S. that have come to us and asked what's your plan, how do you function. We just work together, harvest together, to benefit everyone. People sometimes get greedy, and go away for a few years, but then they figure out they made a mistake, and that we need to work together again.

MK: Very interesting. Thanks again, Dean.

Dean Berden has been farming all his life. He observed the shift from traditional to chemical farming in the 1960s, and transitioned to organic methods in the early 1980s. He is a founding member of Organic Farmers of Michigan. He retired 15 years ago from teaching industrial education and built an off-grid home using solar power. That experience led to a collaboration with his daughter in DB Solar LLC, which provides solar photovoltaic systems to homes, businesses, and farm operations across Michigan. He and his wife continue to grow field crops on their farm in Michigan's Thumb.

MDA Organic Advisory Committee

Julia Christianson

During the 1990s consumer interest in organic food was growing exponentially, and the Michigan Department of Agriculture saw in "organic" the opportunity for a significant boost to the state's agricultural economy. At the same time, the extremely long delay between the passage of the national Organic Foods Production Act in 1990 and the implementation of the "final rule" for organic certification in 2002 created a situation which a number of states, including Michigan, took steps to address.

In September 1998, the Michigan Department of Agriculture (MDA) created the Michigan Organic Advisory Committee. The Committee was charged with developing a strategic plan to serve as a framework for advancing a system for production, processing and marketing the products of organic agriculture in Michigan. The initial committee consisted of 15 members, nine of whom were or would become associated with Organic Growers of Michigan and the Michigan Organic Food and Farm Alliance: Gene Purdum, Sally Page, Shirley Hampshire, Ed Zimba, Merrill Clark, Paul Keiser, Greg Mund, Dan Rossman, and Carol Osborne.

The Committee's first report[1] was issued in June of 1999. Looking at the issue of preserving organic integrity, the report began,

> We recognize the confusion for consumers surrounding the meaning of organic in the marketplace and the need to protect against false labeling, misleading advertising, and

---

[1]   http://worldcat.org/arcviewer/1/EEX/2002/07/30/0000000195/viewer/file18.html

fraudulent practices. We also want to ensure that those growing, processing or handling organic products be certified as complying with certain minimum standards that protect the organic product, from the farm to the consumer.

It is probably fair to say that this was the primary concern of Michigan's organic growers at the time. OGM had been performing organic certification for nearly 30 years, but it was still voluntary, and there was no legal consequence for advertising products as organic even if they were not.

The report recommended a two-fold approach to encouraging the growth of organic farming in Michigan: "Protecting the Industry" by enforcing the integrity of the organic label; and "Promoting the Industry" through a number of approaches, including the formation of a single state-wide trade association or advocacy group, encouraging greater support for organic at Michigan State University, and a continuation of the Advisory Committee's activities until such time as another organization could take its place.

In the absence of national regulations, the Committee's first recommendation was that a regulatory program should be established to "ensure the integrity of products of organic agriculture produced and sold in and/or exported from Michigan"; this resulted in the Organic Products Act passed by the Michigan legislature in 2000.[2]

The Act provided for registration of certification bodies and reciprocity with other states and the Federal government concerning what is to be considered organic. While it incorporated by reference the general standards established by the national Organic Foods Production Act, it also allowed for additional standards to be applied in Michigan,

---

[2]   http://www.legislature.mi.gov/documents/mcl/pdf/mcl-Act-316-of-2000.pdf

and specifically rejected the "big three"—GMOs, sewage sludge, and irradiation—in organic production.[3]

The Act also provided for the continued existence of the Organic Advisory Committee. Its responsibilities were to:

- assist in developing the Michigan organic standards and annually review and recommend changes if necessary;
- review and recommend rules and policies governing the business of organic production and handling by study and evaluation of organic production issues;
- annually conduct or cause to be conducted a comprehensive review of the organic product registration and certifying agent registration programs and advise and recommend to the director any necessary changes to the programs; and
- formulate and recommend to the director actions and policies to promote organic products.

The activities provided for were to be funded through registration fees, and everyone involved was subject to these fees—certifying agencies, processors, handlers, and producers, down to the very small operations making less than $5,000 per year, who were exempt from certification under the federal law. Fees were set on a sliding scale relative to gross receipts, but the combination of the fees and the necessity of paying for certification in order to sell "organic" was an immediate source of resentment for smaller growers.

The mostly small and mid-size growers, the ones who had been the backbone of the organic movement in the years leading up to this point, were also concerned about the very thing that was driving the MDA's interest in organic in these years—their fear was that once government regulations were in place, the major corporations would become involved, and that would mean the end of small scale and local organic production.

---

[3] See page 160 for more on the "big three".

Nevertheless, most of these growers were initially in favor of the Act, because fraud was a real issue. As Pat Whetham wrote in the newsletter in 2000,

> I believe we greatly need this law, as imperfect as it may be. We definitely need a means to deal with the fraud that exists on both a few farms and a number of processors and retails. We in the industry know the fraud exists, but dealing with it effectively without getting sued in the process is a major challenge. For that reason we welcome a law with some teeth in it.

The Act had substantial teeth—penalties ranging from a misdemeanor carrying a $250 fine to a felony conviction involving up to a $10,000 fine and four years in prison for willful violations. But as the decade wore on and enforcement failed to materialize, the larger growers began to resent the fees as well, and the MDA stopped collecting them sometime around 2009.

By 2002, the federal organic rule had been published; it would be fully implemented by October of that year. The existence of the federal standard removed a substantial amount of the impetus for a Michigan organic standard, and over the next few years the problem of goods fraudulently labeled organic diminished as well (though it is still an occasional issue).

But "organic" continued to boom. At the time the Michigan Organic Products Act was passed, MDA Director Dan Wyant said,

> Organic agriculture represents a promising market for Michigan's ag industry as the overall U.S. organic food market is projected to more than triple in value over the next few years.

That projection proved to be true, and during the period 2002-2006 the Organic Advisory Committee continued to meet, and pursue the promotional aspect of its mission. The MDA funded the first Michigan Organic Conferences in 2001 and 2002, held at MSU during ANR Week.

Between 2004 and 2006, Jim Bingen, Carol Osborne, and Emily Reardon conducted a comprehensive study of Michigan organics which contributed to the MDA's objective of study and evaluation of organic business issues.

MDA also provided substantial staff support for organic production and marketing during the early 2000s, in particular with Chris Lietzau as Organic and Sustainable Ag Coordinator. Within a few years, though, the MDA was experiencing budget cuts, and the position of Organic and Sustainable Ag Coordinator was folded into the Division of Pesticide and Pest Management. During this period both Colleen Collier and Robin Rosenbaum of the MDA were active in organic matters to the extent their other obligations permitted.

Toward the middle of the decade, committee meetings became less frequent, and it became increasingly difficult to keep a full complement of members. The committee was finally dissolved by order of the Governor in May of 2007.

(The author wishes to thank Jim Bingen and Carol Osborne for sharing their recollections about the Organic Advisory Committee and the organic movement in the early 2000s.)

Origins of Michigan Land Trustees[1]

Ken Dahlberg

1976 to the 1990s: *Helping to revive traditional organic farming practices and homesteading skills to help spread them throughout Michigan.*

This first section describes the many innovative efforts that MLT pursued through their focus on educating students, local communities, and Western Michigan University about the need either to revive or develop new ways of building healthy soils, growing healthy crops, teaching basic household and small farming skills, while seeking to share that with their home community in Bangor and its immediately surrounding areas.

Michigan Land Trustees had its beginning in 1976 when it was incorporated as a non-profit corporation in the State of Michigan. The original incorporators were Joseph C. Filonowicz, an industrialist from Detroit Michigan who had started a Land Trust in North Carolina, Maynard Kaufman, Western Michigan University Associate Professor of Religion, Paul Shultz, fruit grower-owner of Sunshowers, and Eugene Suchy, Joe's accountant and friend in Detroit. The Articles of Incorporation were written by Joe Filonowicz. MLT's by-laws were written by Paul Shultz and Maynard Kaufman.

---

[1] This overview draws upon the 10th and the 30th anniversary MLT Newsletters—which are available at http://www.michigan landtrust.org—plus an incomplete set of documents available to me. My hope is that the collage of activities, reports, and events presented here will give you a clear picture of MLT's vitality and evolution.

After exploring various types of tax exempt status, the IRS gave MLT provisional 509(a)(1) status in 1977 to do the following:

1. "scientific testing, evaluation and demonstration of 'Appropriate Technologies' suitable to the development of local self-reliance under conditions of petroleum and natural gas scarcity."

2. "educating the agricultural community in ecological and energy-conserving agricultural production and the public in energy conservation in general. And in addition, to: train individuals in the techniques of agriculture production which are ecologically sound." and finally that

3. "Your other activities will include the establishment of a 'living-learning' homesteading school which will operate in conjunction with Western Michigan University."

Once MLT was recognized as a tax-exempt organization, Joe Filonowicz donated to MLT a 38 acre run-down, junk-strewn farm north of Bangor just up the road from Maynard and Sally Kaufman's "School of Homesteading". This was to be the setting for the WMU Homesteading Program. Maynard and Sally had operated a similar living-learning "School of Homesteading" on their own since 1973 and continued to work with "apprentices" in succeeding decades.

As designated "Homesteading Coordinator" Maynard also managed the complex relationship between WMU and MLT. In 1979, a year after a temporary instructor for the "Land Trust Homesteading Farm" (LTHF) completed his tasks, Jon Towne took over as instructor and continued to manage this living-learning farm where resident students were taught small-scale farming, food production, preserving, and alternative energy until 1983. At that point, Thom Phillips and Jan Filonowicz took over for a year, after which Jon Towne and Bobbi Martindale decided to lease the farm. Later on they purchased the farm on a land contract from MLT (see below).

While the homesteading program was a central activity of MLT during those early years, there were other projects. In 1977, Maynard brought MLT and Environmental Studies Program faculty members at WMU together to offer a series of programs at the Kalamazoo Nature Center focused on the topic: "The Pastoral Ideal and the New Homesteading Movement". Also, MLT offered a series of public workshops during this time and in succeeding years that were designed to help people acquire skills for self-reliance.

In 1979, Sally Kaufman became the first MLT news-letter editor, with two to three issues coming out each year. Shortly before her untimely death in 1990 Sally gave up her editorship to Michael Phillips, who served in that capacity through 2000, when Jon Towne took over as editor.

In 1980, a new Dean of Arts and Sciences at WMU cut all funding for the Homesteading Program. Even so, Maynard and Sally continued to offer their program and MLT assumed responsibility for conducting the homestead-ing courses at the Land Trust Homesteading Farm.

The interests of Joe Filonowicz went beyond the land trust and homesteading programs to issues relating to community revitalization, and in 1979 he organized a new arm of MLT called "Community Connections." It was focus-ed on the improvement of business and social life in the Bangor area. Robert Holmes was hired for the better part of a year to carry out these programs.

In 1981 Board member Sally Kaufman worked with the City of Bangor to organize a garden project in Bangor. Garden plots were provided by the city and Sally offered advice to those who wanted to grow vegetables. This continued for several years.

In 1982, with a grant secured by Maynard from the Michigan Council of Humanities, MLT organized a day long workshop called: "Condos, Cornfields, and Homesteads: The New Rural Residents and Land Use." It was presented in Paw Paw and several faculty members from WMU and Michigan State University made presentations.

As enrollments in the homesteading program declined in the early 1980s, MLT began to shift its thinking and

OGM-MLT Field Day, 1981

focus to permaculture, seen then as perhaps a more evolved and sophisticated form of homesteading and organic farming. Jon Towne developed a rudimentary permaculture plan for the Land Trust Homesteading Farm. Some aspects of this plan were implemented on the farm with tree plantings and structural changes.

In 1985, a three-week "Great Lakes Permaculture Design Course"—one of the first permaculture courses taught in Michigan—took place on the Land Trust Homesteading Farm. Taught by Dan Hemenway, ten students received their Permaculture Design Certificate after developing a much more elaborate version of Jon's earlier plan. In 1986, Dan returned to teach a weekend workshop.

During the rest of the '80s, Jon utilized this newly acquired knowledge to prepare and present a number of permaculture slide shows to several groups. Over the following years and decades he also has implemented many elements of the original plan. While Jon and Bobbi have not managed the farm with the with a goal of self-sufficiency, they do grow and preserve much of their food, utilize tree crops, and generally provide a model for living "lightly on the land". Jon has also continued planting indigenous trees—some 500 of them this spring!

In 1987, MLT and Organic Growers of Michigan (southwest chapter) sponsored a Country Skills Workshop. As part of its emphasis on tree planting, trees were given out at Earth Day Events in 1990s. Also in the early 90s a "Local Exchange Trading System" (LETS) system to enable people with different skills to "trade" them was started in Bangor. Although it attracted and helped nearly 50 partici-pants for a couple of years, it did not achieve the "critical mass" needed to continue.

The 1990s to early 2000s: *Seeking to broaden the organic movement's audiences through new programs, organiza-tions, and coalitions.*

The early part of this period was one of introspection flowing in part from the collapse of the LETS system and the minimal results from some community-building projects that Joe Filonowicz had promoted. More important was the increasing lack of student interest in taking homesteading courses on the Land Trust Homesteading Farm. Adapting to these changes, Jon and Bobbi decided to submit an offer to purchase the LTHF property. An assessment was made to determine the market value. The Board accepted this and the details of a land contract sale were worked out in 1994.

This infusion of monthly money allowed MLT to become, in effect, a small "local foundation" in Southwest Michigan. How best to use this money led to several brainstorming meetings of the Board. To focus the discussions, MLT Chairperson Ken Dahlberg suggested four possible options for the future of the organization: 1) Buy another piece of property; 2) Help set up an ecological community near an urban area that would emphasize alternative energy and self-sufficiency; 3) Donate most of MLT's now increased assets to similar organizations, while maintaining a small budget to continue the newsletter and hold meetings; and 4) Disband MLT and donate its assets to like-minded organizations.

The result of these discussions was that MLT decided to receive proposals for worthy projects supporting MTL's sustainability and local community resilience-building goals as well as to provide funds and seed money for emerging and promising local organizations. The initial effort began with a large donation to the Michigan Organic Food and Farm Alliance (http://www.moffa.net). Its mission is "to promote the development of food systems that rely on organic methods of food production and that revitalize and sustain local communities." Other grants to MOFFA have been approved in the years since, bringing the total donated to MOFFA to some $19,000.

In 1994 MLT sought to save WMU's Lee Baker Farm from being developed into a "Business, Research, and Technology Park." Representing MLT, Ken Dahlberg unsuccessfully lobbied to have it zoned for "renewable and green space." Such zoning would have permitted: 1) sustainable agriculture and/or forestry; 2) community gardens; 3) educational uses directly related to the character of the land; and 4) passive recreation.

In 1997, MLT created its own world-wide-web presence—http://www.michiganlandtrust.org—with Jon Towne as its webmaster.

In 1998, much planning went into organizing a summer reunion of homesteading students from the Kaufman's School of Homesteading and the Land Trust Homesteading Farm. It lived up to expectations as can be seen in a wide variety of event essays and pictures that can be found on MLT's website.

Early 2000s to 2010: *Working with local and state food and environmental groups to: 1) help them understand the centrality of local sustainable and organic farming to their own concerns; and 2) to encourage them to help restore our depleted soils. It also became clear at this point that it was time to revise our mission statement and brochure.*

On March 2, 2003, Kalamazoo People's Food Co-op submitted a request to help create its Kalamazoo Community Gardens Initiative. MLT provided $500.

Later in 2003, MOFFA, represented by Maynard Kaufman, organized the first annual Southwest Michigan Harvest Festival. MLT voted to fund a minimum $1,000 pending a detailed budget report. The first Southwest Michigan Harvest Fest was held at Tillers International (www.tillersinternational.org). MLT, along with other local groups and foundations, has provided generous support each year since then. In 2015, Tillers took over the task of organizing and running the Fest.

The summer and early autumn of 2004 were spent in long term prioritizing and budgeting. Topics included promoting CSAs, making land available for farming, as well as learning how to donate and/or receive development rights. The Van Buren MSU Cooperative Extension Service related their experience with township and municipal planning that included provisions for open-space preservation. A committee was established to explore the feasibility of developing synergistic relationships with established preservation groups. As it turned out, a variety of differences were found that made that unlikely.

In 2005, Ken Dahlberg, Jim Bingen from MOFFA, and Kami Pothukuchi of Wayne State, with some MLT support for printing costs, completed *Healthy People, Places, and Communities: A 2025 Vision for Michigan's Food and Farming*. Its goals were: 1) to provide food security for all; 2) to promote sustainable family farms in ways that would provide a significant portion of Michigan's food; 3) create healthier, more self-reliant communities and cities built upon meaningful livelihoods for all; and 4) provide healthy air, clean waters, and healthy soils and habitats throughout the state. A website "The Citizens Network for Michigan Food Democracy" was created with the hope of recruiting a good number of activists to promote implementation of the various goals in the vision statement. It can be viewed at: http://homepages.wmich.edu/~dahlberg/mifooddem/. There are hopeful signs that its focus on state-level advocacy and policy making is gaining more interest.

In 2006, MLT made a $1000 donation to help support the work of the Growing Matters Garden program in Kalamazoo through the fall and winter. In spring 2007, GMG Manager Heather Crull wrote that MLT's generous donation had helped them to cover a portion of the costs of completing an important program evaluation as part of developing a garden-based curriculum for one of Kalamazoo Public School's magnet schools, Woodward School for Technology and Research (WSTaR), as well as developing long-term fundraising strategies.

During the summer of 2009 the MLT Board decided to offer public tours of the farms and gardens of most of the

MLT Board members. The goal was to help the public learn more about how to connect better with the land, plants, animal life and the environment.

2009 was the year that, after a number of meetings and lots of discussion, we revised our mission statement and brochure as follows: "Convinced that healthy connections and relationships between people, plant, and animal life and the environment are the source of the resilience needed to adapt to peak oil and climate chaos ... Michigan Land Trustees has dedicated itself to the goal of revitalizing sustainable rural and urban communities by promoting responsible land use and the development of local food and energy systems."

2010 to the present: *MLT has sought to increase its organizational presence at all levels to encourage a greater awareness of the global need to try to reduce the clear and hugely disruptive threats to the earth and its peoples from the ongoing burning of fossil fuels. Important contributions in reducing these threats can be made by seeking to close the carbon cycle. This is best done by returning the carbon emissions to our soils, pastures, and forests—something that will require the replacement of fossil-fuel based chemical agriculture, grazing, and plantation forestry with regenerative organic farming, grazing, and forestry that sequesters the carbon and helps restore lost soils and create humus.*

To give you a sense of the different facets involved in pursuing the above goals, here's a summary of three different—but overlapping—approaches that MLT members and friends have pursued:

APPROACH NUMBER 1: Focus on local skills and community-based approaches that seek new ways to combine their knowledge of useful skills and find ways to pass them on to their neighbors, their local communities, as well as to different groups and existing organizations. This can also be done with groups, such as "Transition" communities, that are seeking to create communities with greater self-reliance in the face of climate change. Often, they also include a strong desire to share their knowledge with the next generation. Some examples include:

- Rita and Norm Bober's successful work in setting up the Lawton Community Garden, which has helped in getting fresh and healthy food to both interested as well as needy people. They also worked with the Transition community in Lawton locate, publish, and put on the web a "Local Lawton Food and Farm Guide."

- Maynard's work on a day-long reskilling program at the Bangor Community Education Center, part of which focused on the City's community garden project. He also worked with TVBA (Transition Van Buren & Allegan). With MLT support, they created an attractive and informative brochure. Unfortunately, interest and participation declined and led to their dissolution. Their funds were distributed to somewhat more successful Transitions groups in South Haven, Lawton, and Kalamazoo.

APPROACH NUMBER 2: Focus on enhancing existing educational programs to enrich their programs as well as to reach out to new groups and/or areas. Here MLT helped various local, city-wide and/or regional level organizations:

- MLT helped create the Greater Grand Rapids Food Systems Council by funding a day-long visioning session and providing early operational visits and advice.

- Early on, MLT supported the creation of Fair Food Matters, whose mission it was to educate Kalamazoo about its different food systems. In turn, FFM helped create the Good Food Kalamazoo Coalition GFK), which MLT joined. In 2011, GFK organized and presented two panels on Kalamazoo food systems at the MI Downtown Assn. meetings held in Kalamazoo that year. After that—and with some staff support from FFM—it also organized a major meeting for a variety of local non-profits to help educate them on our local food systems.

Several successful monthly brown bag networking lunches were also conducted. GFK was also able to carry out some modest programs held in conjunction with the 2013 visit from the renowned climate activist, Bill McKibben, founder of 350.org.

- In 2014 FFM was disbanded. MLT then acted to salvage the two remaining—and successful—operational programs of FFM: 1) MLT provided a grant to The Can-Do Kitchen to pay the legal costs of obtaining non-profit status and having its own website. 2) MLT supported the other very successful and ongoing FFM program— the Growing Matters Garden (GMG)—by ensuring that it "inherited" FFM's website and legal status as a non-profit organization. This action strengthened GMG, its garden, and its teaching programs.

APPROACH NUMBER 3: This involved what became the title of a pre-conference field trip for interested Agriculture, Food, and Human Values members who wanted to visit five MLT-related organically farmed properties. Ken and Maynard helped Laura DeLind of MSU and Taylor Reid of MOFFA to organize the 2013 tour—which was extremely well received by a very diverse audience. The title of the field trip was Passing Organic Farmland to the Next Generation, a Southwest Michigan Eutopia. A detailed summary with photos is available at: http://www.michigan landtrust.org/BangorFieldTrip.pdf.

This was more than a wonderful tour; it celebrated the sale of most of the 160 acres of the School of Homesteading Farm to three younger farmers, including two organic vegetable growers. It also enabled Maynard and Barbara to finance construction of a new off-the-grid house on a part of the acreage they now called "Sunflower Farm". Thom Phillips was the chief designer and builder. This resulted in a very energy efficient home and also gave Thom the practical experience to become the "Green Building Coordinator" for Habitat Michigan. The overall result of this gradual process has been the creation of a strong multigenerational community of adjacent land owners who grow and/or raise organic crops, trees, and animals.

In summary, in its forty years, Michigan Land Trustees has played an important role in educating students, facilitating the creation of a range of innovative and effective new organizations, and expanding and deepening the knowledge and capabilities of almost all groups involved in the organic movement in Michigan. Given the depth of change needed to address increasing climate changes as well as to help restructure and regenerate our sources of healthy food and farming, MLT can be expected to continue to play a significant and creative role.

Dr. Kenneth A. Dahlberg is Distinguished Professor Emeritus of Political Science, Environmental and Sustainability Studies. His academic re-search and writing has regularly gone into areas not previously explored. This started with his 1979 book, Beyond the Green Revolution: The Ecology and Politics of Global Agricultural Development *and was followed in 1986 with* New Directions for Agriculture and Agricultural Research: Neglected Dimensions and Emerging Alternatives. *His inter-est in research and policy development led to two Kellogg Foundation grants: "Building a National Network of Municipal Food System Policy Groups" 1994-1997. In 1982, he was elected a Fellow of the American Association for the Advancement of Science. He served on the Agriculture, Forestry, and Waste Technical Work Group of Gov. Granholm's Climate Action Council 2008-2009. He helped the Greater Grand Rapids Food Council get started and served as the MLT representative to the Good Food Kalamazoo Coalition.*

Community Supported Agriculture in 2002: The State of the Art in Michigan [1]

Laura B. DeLind

Many people, individually and collectively, are seeking alternative arrangements for producing and consuming life-giving food and fiber. They want to escape the clutches of industrial agriculture and find a safer, more secure food supply. One model that has captured local and regional imagination is community supported agriculture (CSA).

CSA allows local farmers and local residents to interact around the production of fresh produce. Farmers grow food for community members, not for distant markets. CSA members, in turn, support the efforts of small-scale farmers, sometimes physically as well as financially. By investing in "one's own" farm and "one's own" farmer *before* the season begins, members offer to share the risks and rewards of food production. It is a compelling first step toward supporting small-scale, diversified farming, restoring local economies and food self-reliance, and revitalizing citizenship and communities of place.

In 1998, a SARE-funded study surveyed the CSAs in OH, MI, and IN. The publication, *The Many Faces of Community Supported Agriculture*, profiled dozens of these small, diversified and labor-intensive enterprises. While

---

[1] This chapter begins with excerpts from an article written in 2002 by Dr. Laura B. DeLind, as a follow-up to a study she conducted in 1998. The full text of the 2002 article is available online at www.moffa.net/f/Community-Supported-Agriculture-in-2002.pdf. A few words from Julia Christianson on the state of Community Supported Agriculture in Michigan as of 2016 conclude the chapter.

each operation was clearly unique, as a group they followed organic practices, encouraged farmer-consumer interaction, and sought ways to reintegrate food and farming into community life. What has happened to them, and to CSA generally, over the course of the last four years?

Prompted by these questions, we decided to resurvey CSAs in OH, MI, and IN.[2] Our purpose was two-fold. First we wanted to up-date basic CSA data for this region of the Midwest (and especially for Michigan). How many of the original CSAs still existed, how many new ones had appeared? Did they exhibit any new characteristics? Second, we wanted to know what types of resources and assistance CSAs needed. What would help them grow more numerous, visible and viable?

We located thirty-two CSAs in Michigan, a number that includes the original eight found in 1998. We were able to interview twenty-nine CSAs, or about 90%. We found that two CSAs from the original group of eight had quit and one was taking the year off to reorganize. Of those new since 1998,[3] three were no longer operating as CSAs. In total, we interviewed twenty-three working CSAs, five defunct CSAs, and one "resting" CSA.

Michigan CSAs have been in existence between one and fifteen years, with an average of 3.9 years. The newest group of CSAs, those 1-2 years old, contains considerable demographic and economic variation. Six are being farmed by persons—several with young families—who depend on agriculture for the bulk of their household income. Four

---

[2] This survey was made possible by a grant from the National Farmers Union and the Michigan Farmers Union Foundation. The author would like to thank Vicki Morrone, Tara Hefferan and most especially Heather Van Wormer for their assistance.

[3] The original 1998 survey missed at least two CSAs that had been operating for several years. These are included in the "new" (i.e. since 1998) group for the purpose of "a nose count" and to avoid confusion.

are being managed by individuals who are retired or are approaching retirement age. The remaining three CSAs are connected to 501(c)(3) organizations and through them to the issues of public welfare.

The growing season for Michigan CSAs averages between 18 and 22 weeks. For the majority of CSAs, a "full share" is designed for a household of four persons. Well over half of Michigan's CSAs also offer half shares. As one experienced grower observed, "What we provided for a family of four is now what a family of eight or twelve would use. [People] are not self-provisioning." Time is certainly a factor here, but as people spend less time storing, processing and cooking their own food, they lose the knowledge and skills to do so. Without the skills to manage, even the most sympathetic CSA member can be burdened with produce (as well as a sense of guilt). These burdens, in turn, directly affect the way in which CSAs are able to operate as producers, educators, and system reformers.

Michigan CSAs provide a cornucopia of seasonal vegetables. Many also provide herbs, cutting flowers, berries, maple syrup and/or fruit. Thirteen CSAs offer meat or animal products (e.g., wool, lamb, fish, poultry, eggs, honey), or specialty food items (e.g., stone milled bread, mushrooms) to members.

Because of the growing number of share options, share prices are more varied now than they were four years ago, They are also noticeably higher. Currently, full shares for 18-22 weeks average $445/share. The cost in 1998, by comparison, averaged $400/share. Few low income residents are active members of CSAs and with one notable exception, no Michigan CSA expressly welcomes low income families as participants within the farm-centered community.

Today, as was also true in 1998, the majority of shares (14) are picked up at the farm, and only at the farm.

However, there are more farms that offer an off-farm pick up option now than four years ago (11 vs. 3). In 2002, as in 1998, it is the farmer who expends the time and labor to harvest and/or pack individual distribution baskets, bags and boxes. In only one new CSA and one original CSA do members pick and pack their own weekly shares; both of these CSAs distribute shares only on-farm and both have work requirements for members.

With respect to membership work requirements, five of the original eight CSAs had working shares or mandatory work requirements; two of these had ceased to exist by 2002. Of the new CSAs, nine experimented with working shares or work requirements. Of these, one CSA folded and three have experienced difficulty getting members to follow through on their on-farm work commitments.

One of the hallmarks of CSA is its ability to share production and financial risk among farmers and farm members. Members accept, along with the grower, the shortfalls and windfalls that come with farming in cooperation with nature. Theoretically, at least, members are not purchasing vegetables, but investing in a more organic or sustainable way of life. But, theory and practice do not necessarily coincide. For many members (and even a few growers) the CSA relationship easily reduces to that of buying and selling a quality product—the exchange of "x" number of dollars for "y" amount of produce.

It is extremely difficult to alter this economic reality and mind set. CSA growers who are drawn to a more humanly-scaled and community-oriented enterprise are caught on the horns of a dilemma. To make a living, they are required to compete with the conventional food system; at the same time, they are required to assume social and educational roles that will hopefully help to re-value and re-form that system. CSA farmers write newsletters, organize farm tours and potlucks, offer canning classes, and speak publicly about the benefits of a local food system—activities designed to educate and recruit members. Fitting these activities into the already labor intensive routine of organic farming can easily lead to self-exploitation and burnout. As an ex-CSA farmer admitted, "The one thing that pushed me out of it—it took all the time I had."

Members, however, are under no such obligation to extend themselves. Overall, the trend seems to be toward regularizing and narrowing the farmer-member relationship, a pattern consistent with shareholders being called "customers" and "subscribers" (as opposed to "members" or "shareholders") in at least six of the new CSAs.

Moving distribution sites off the farm has a similar effect. On the one hand, it allows farmers to serve a wider geographic area and combine CSA produce delivery with other marketing activities (e.g., farmers markets). On the other hand, this "off-farm connection" together with the absence of an on-farm work requirement, weakens a member's engagement with the CSA. While such behavior is understandable from a risk management standpoint, it reinforces more market-like farmer-member relations.

In 2002, as in 1998, all Michigan CSAs stated that they believed in and followed organic farming practices. In 2002, however, the issue of certification has become a concern for many growers. Nine CSA growers indicate that they are certified organic or will apply for certification for three basic reasons. First, some view certification and maintaining national standards as a way to politically support the organic movement. Second, some believe that certification will help them attract more members and allow them to charge higher prices for their produce. Third, because CSA growers may also sell to farmers markets, restaurants, etc. they need a third party seal to use the "O" word and to vouch for the quality of their produce.

Those who see no reason to certify (15) also have three main arguments. Politically, some feel that the codification of the organic process serves large scale commercial interests—that organic has been reduced to a finite set of materials and techniques that can be owned and controlled by national and transnational corporations. Others find that certification is simply too expensive. Most, however, feel that certification is simply irrelevant because CSA members can "see for themselves" how their food is being grown.

When CSA farmers were asked what type of assistance they needed, their primary response was "education"—both *public education* and *self education*. With respect to public education, CSA farmers wanted the public-at-large to understand the "corruption" and the contradictions that exist within the present food system. They wanted people to understand that local organic was not the same as corporate organic—environmentally, nutritionally, or ethically. Several farmers bluntly stated that "people don't care about what they eat as long as their stomachs are full."

With respect to self education, sixteen farmers saw a need for an annual conference. CSA farmers also wanted MSU to conduct more research into "smaller-scale, diversified production." They wanted information on scale appropriate and ergonomically appropriate tools, on food crop storage, on creating niche products. One farmer wanted research on the economic viability of CSA. "Is there a good economic model out there or not?" he asked. "Is this a way to make a decent living for people?" Another farmer saw the need for an independent, possibly state-wide, program that would serve as a clearing house for trained interns. Others saw the need for traveling workshops to present information on a variety of topics, but especially on multi-farm CSAs. Another farmer wanted more local organic suppliers, sources for potting soil, sprays and amendments. It was felt that a MACSAC[4]-like organization could coordinate these needs and facilitate the sharing of equipment, seed orders, transportation, etc. among farms.

These suggestions for assistance reflect not only the growing diversity of Michigan CSAs, but also an awareness on the part of CSA growers of their growing presence within the state. No longer curiosities, CSAs are gaining a sense of their collective identity—and their collective strength. CSA advocates already demonstrate a sophistication and a willingness to address their needs and to help themselves. What they feel they need is a non-governmental, not-for-profit organization that can speak for CSAs generally and coordinate many of their on-farm needs and extra-farm responsibilities. Finding the most appropriate model, one that will protect the integrity of diverse, small, place-based enterprises *and* craft and coordinate friendly state-level programs and policies, will require considerable dialogue and negotiation. The challenge now will be to bring interested CSA farmers, members, and community residents together to get the process rolling.

CSA Development Since 2002

Julia Christianson

In the 14 years since 2002, Community Supported Agriculture has continued to grow and change. Increasing diversity of items included as part of a CSA share, as well as variations in the size and character of shares, continues.

---

[4] Madison Area Community Supported Agriculture Coalition (now [2017] the FairShare CSA Coalition).

The shift from member-contributed labor to a more traditional buyer/seller relationship is nearly complete. The great majority of CSA operations in 2017 are single farm to consumer relationships, but a few multi-farm and 501(c)(3) CSAs continue to exist.

There is still no comprehensive list of CSAs, so it is not possible to say with any certainty how many CSAs exist in Michigan today. However, several organizations maintain lists. By far the largest is Local Harvest, a database started in 2000 to help consumers connect with producers who are local to them. Dr. DeLind consulted Local Harvest, as well as other sources, to arrive at a total of 32 CSAs in Michigan in 2002. Today, Local Harvest lists 305 CSAs in Michigan, 158 of which use the word "organic" in their description. In 2012, Erin Barnett of Local Harvest estimated that their database includes 65% to 70% of all of the CSAs in the U.S. The Robyn Van En Center at Wilson College currently lists 77 CSAs in Michigan; the USDA Directory of Community Supported Agriculture has 40; and MOFFA's Farm Guide lists 49—and each of these lists contains farms which do not appear on any of the other lists.

In 2002, the regulations governing USDA Organic certification were just beginning to be implemented, so the question of whether to become USDA certified was common. At that time, 38% of those interviewed indicated they currently were or were planning to become certified, and all indicated that they believed in and followed organic practices. Today, 63% of the CSAs in MOFFA's Farm Guide are USDA certified, and all are growing using organic principles, whether certified or not. However, we cannot say how many of the 305 CSAs listed at Organic Harvest are growing in a sustainable manner. In any event, the reasons for and against seeking certification are largely the same today as they were in 2002.

At the time of the 2002 survey, Dr. DeLind identified clustering of CSAs in several distinct regions (e.g. Traverse City, Detroit, and Ann Arbor). MOFFA's 2016 Farm Guide shows a cluster around Traverse City (and a very small cluster in the U.P.), but a fairly even distribution across the southern half of the lower peninsula.

CSA Operations in MOFFA's Farm Guide, 2016

Organic Food Co-ops in Michigan: A Case History of Oryana Community Co-op

Luise Bolleber

Like yogurt and granola, food co-ops and organic food go hand in hand. Food co-ops aren't just hip places to shop for healthy, organic food and vitamins. Co-ops played an important role in changing the way we thought about food production in the latter part of the 20th century and spawned a thriving natural foods industry. In fact, co-ops directly contributed to the development of the national organic standards in the late 1990s. This is not surprising given the environmentally aware, conscientious nature of food co-ops.

Michigan was one of many states whose citizens responded to the social and environmental upheaval of the 1960s and 70s by forming food buying clubs, which evolved into member-owned food cooperatives. Many of these are still going strong today, however the earliest beginnings of cooperatives go all the way back to 19th century England.

The Rochdale Cooperative, founded in 1844 in Rochdale, England, was not the first ever cooperative business, but it was considered to be the most well known and successful. The industrial revolution was well under way by the 1840s, a time when adults and children slaved in factories and mines for 12 hours a day. People endured wretched living conditions, low wages, debtors' prison, and many other indignities. Adulteration of foods was a common practice by many shopkeepers of that day. They added water to milk, alum to flour, potatoes to flour, even ground limestone to flour. These harsh realities spurred a few forward thinking men to fight for a better life. A group of

28 weavers and other tradespeople banded together to open their own store selling pure foods at honest prices. With pooled money they purchased butter, sugar, flour, oatmeal and tallow candles. They named their organization the Rochdale Society of Equitable Pioneers.

When the Pioneers took a stand against exploitation and opened for business in an old rented warehouse on December 21, 1844, the longest night of the year, they ushered in a revolutionary approach to a brighter future, not only for themselves but for the generations that followed. Their enlightened venture was the beginning of the modern cooperative movement.

In the United States, a wave of co-op development began in the early 1900s, followed by a surge in the 1930s. With a few exceptions such as Hanover Co-op in New Hampshire, Eau Claire Co-op in Wisconsin, and Hyde Park Co-op in New York, most of the earliest co-ops did not survive.

Another wave of co-ops gathered strength in the 1960s when the youth of America were disillusioned with the war in Vietnam. Civil rights grievances and environmental concerns bubbled up, especially after Rachel Carson published her book *Silent Spring*, exposing the hazards of DDT.

The tensions of this era birthed "The Hippies" subculture. The Hippies were mistrustful of the processed food industry and factory farms. They had grown up eating meat, potatoes, Twinkies, and Wonder Bread but began to understand the true cost of these foods. They rejected chemical-laden, processed foods and turned instead toward whole, local, and organic foods. In Warren Belasco 's book *Appetite for Change — How the Counterculture Took on the Food Industry*, the author discusses the overarching conflict between citizens and those that controlled the food supply. "There was a conspiracy of agribusiness firms, medical professionals, and government officials. When experts brushed aside Carson's evidence on DDT, Adelle Davis' qualms about additives, or the Rodale Press' concerns about organic farming, it seemed clear that a systematic cover-up was in progress," he states. The ecology movement Carson helped start corroborated the values of the Hippies, namely that food production and consumption directly impacts the environment. People were learning that by eating natural and organic foods, they could reduce their ecological footprint.

Just like the Rochdale Pioneers, small groups of people all over the U.S., including Michigan, began forming buying clubs in order to purchase the kinds of wholesome foods they couldn't find in grocery stores. The staples of brown rice, tofu, granola, whole wheat bread, yogurt, and sprouts, for which Hippies endured scorn, were foreign to mainstream America. These kinds of foods, in addition to organic produce, effectively rejected conventional American cuisine and formed the core offerings of buying clubs. Oryana Community Co-op in Traverse City was one such buying club. According to Joe Tiedeck, one of Oryana's founding members, they were supporting an alternative food structure and bringing people closer to the source of food. "There was ownership and identification of what we were eating," he said.

Joe became interested in obtaining natural foods because of the politics of the time. "It was a way of expressing my politics in a concrete way," he said. "The basic necessity of food was a natural fit. Taking this basic necessity and getting involved in the procurement and distribution of food was a perfect match. It was a way of getting out of the profit channel. Through the buying club we created economic and quality control over the food we did buy."

The idea for a buying club emerged at a community alternative forum sponsored by the local crisis center, Third Level. Joe, along with David Milarch, Jim Crockett, and

ten other families, established the club in the community
room behind the Michigan Consolidated Gas Company
office. "All we had back then was Oleson's and Prevo's
[grocery stores]. There were no whole foods anywhere in
the region unless you went to someone's farm," remembered
David Milarch. Jim Crockett also recalled the scarcity of

Co-op members Maggie Zimmerman, Kathy Moyer-Weber,
Linda Grigg, Eric Bartell, and Tom Slater in the
mid-1980s at the Oryana food production facility.

natural foods. "You couldn't even buy whole wheat flour or
whole grains back then. I was 30 and my wife was
pregnant with our first child. My wife was really keen on
eating naturally. We grew our own food. I was grinding
our own wheat berries with a Quaker hand-cranked mill."

The foods that the first members wanted—peanut
butter with no additives, good quality cheese, whole wheat
flour, dry beans, whole grains, sea salt—were only available downstate in Ann Arbor at the People's Food Co-op,
which was wholesaling to other co-ops around the state.
"We made our first run to Ann Arbor in Joe's old Econoline

Ford van that had no heat. We distributed it in an un-heated single car garage on 16th street. I brought my farm scales to use. It was so cold in that garage," Milarch re-called.

Like other young co-ops in Michigan, Oryana hop-scotched to different locations as it grew. As more folks joined the club it moved to two different members' back porches. There was a move to a more commercial area near downtown and then a permanent home in downtown Traverse City. This location had 600 square feet of space on the second floor. Oryana officially incorporated as a co-op on June 18, 1973 and an all-volunteer staff provided the labor. By this time the organization required someone to be in charge of the daily operation and Christopher Morey became the first manager. Oryana even had a live-in vol-unteer, David Poinsett, who slept on the floor in his sleeping bag.

For the first year, volunteers made the weekly trek to Ann Arbor for supplies. Eventually, the People's Co-op wholesale operation evolved into the Michigan Federation of Food Co-ops, which ran its own mill and warehouse, sell-ing Michigan-grown organic grains, beans and flour to co-ops nationwide. Oryana then started receiving truck deliv-eries rather than sending volunteers to the downstate warehouse. It was all hands on deck when the truck arrived. "I remember the long staircase on Front Street," Jim Crockett recalled. "Someone would call me up and tell me the truck is on the way and I'd go and help if it was my turn. I carried 100 pound bags up those stairs." To keep track of inventory, a giant green chalkboard listed all the prices of products. By 1975 Oryana's sales were at $15,000.

Oryana's first big crisis occurred in 1977 when thieves robbed the store and made off with all the working capital, about $2000 in cash. The staff had foolishly neglected to make regular nightly deposits, electing instead to hide the money in a bucket of dried beans. The loss of this money presented a real threat to Oryana's survival, but David Poinsett, among others, made sure this did not happen. Dave, who by then had moved out and gotten another job, quit his job to work at Oryana 60 hours a week and do everything in his power to keep it afloat. He paid himself $1 an hour. (The minimum wage that year was $2.30 per hour.) Oryana did manage to survive and interest in natural foods continued to grow.

Mike Williams, Oryana General Manager, 1980

Oryana made its next major move in 1980 when it purchased a building close to downtown. The purchase price was $96,000 under a land contract at 10% interest with a $24,000 down payment. Co-ops were not considered good financial risks at that time but Oryana was fortunate to be the first in the nation to secure a loan from the National Cooperative Bank. In 1997 Oryana moved again to its current location, still within the city limits. Several renovations and expansions later (on the same property), Oryana is still going strong with over $16 million in sales and is the largest co-op in Michigan.

Michigan boasts eight other co-ops that all started in a similar fashion as Oryana in the early 1970s:

- Keweenaw Co-op in Hancock debuted in 1973 and is Michigan's northern-most co-op on Copper Island in the Keweenaw Peninsula.
- Marquette Food Co-op in Marquette opened its doors in 1971 and celebrated a grand re-opening in 2014 in a bright, new space in downtown Marquette.

- Ypsilanti Food Co-op in Ypsilanti opened in 1975 and now has 10,000 feet of space including the co-op bakery that features a wood-fired oven.

- The People's Food Co-op in Ann Arbor was founded in 1971 by two University of Michigan students and is located in the Kerrytown shopping district.

- East Lansing Food Co-op (ELFCO) in East Lansing started in 1976 but ceased the storefront operation in January 2017 in the face of severe sales declines. They are actively pursuing a reimagining and transformation with the goal of eventually reopening.

- Green Tree Cooperative Grocery in Mt. Pleasant started in 1970 and is currently searching for a new location with plans to expand to three times its current size.

- People's Food Co-op Natural Grocery and Deli in Kalamazoo incorporated in 1973 and also operates three farmers markets in the area.

- Grain Train Natural Foods Market in Petoskey got started in 1971 and operates a thriving store in downtown Petoskey. They also opened a second, smaller store in Boyne City in 2013.

Other co-ops in Michigan include Northwind Natural Foods Co-op in Ironwood, Ionia Natural Foods Co-op in Ionia, Livingston Organic Food Co-op in Brighton, Hillsdale Natural Grocery in Hillsdale, and Michigan's newest co-op, opened in 2016, Community Vibrations in Jackson.

Food buying clubs in Michigan (listed on coopdirectory .org) include Authentic Provisions in Ann Arbor, Brighton Food Co-op in Brighton, Dibbleville Food Co-op in Fenton, Sturgeon River Co-op in Wolverine, West Michigan Co-op in Grand Rapids (online co-op), and Woodland Food Co-op in Woodland.

Three other Michigan co-ops are in the planning stages: The Grand Rapids Food Co-op, the Detroit People's Food Co-op, and Bay City Cooperative Market in Bay City.

Co-ops and the development of organic standards

Oregon passed the first state law regulating organic food in 1973, thus providing the impetus for other states to follow suit. Stakeholders in the organic industry struggled to define what organic food was and to standardize growing methods. Many states lacked any organic food statutes at all and producers and marketers were able to make unfounded organic claims. The patchwork of organic food regulations made consumers have to guess at what was truly organic and what was not. Finally, in the late 1980s, the organic industry petitioned the U.S. Congress, asking it to draft legislation that would clearly define "organic".

In 1990 Congress passed the Organic Foods Production Act, which designated the USDA to establish the definition of organic. In order to assist the USDA in developing the regulation, OFPA provided that a National Organic Standards Board (NOSB) would be assembled to serve as an advisory board.

When the NOSB proposed the first organic regulations in 1997 it faced a huge public outcry. The proposal endorsed techniques such as irradiation, genetic modification, and sewage sludge fertilization. Organic farmers, co-ops, and advocacy groups were outraged at the USDA's proposal. The USDA received over 275,000 comments during a public comment period, which included comments from Oryana and other food co-ops.

"What's up with that appalling rule proposed by the USDA that would have made the term "organic" a joke?" reads an article in a 1998 Oryana newsletter. Sandi McArthur, Education and Outreach Coordinator at Oryana, remembered commenting on the rule. "We commented as a co-op," she said. "Co-ops were good about getting information to members to comment. We've always been a big proponent of organic food, even before we had our strict buying guidelines." The newsletter article features a long letter that Oryana sent to the USDA, detailing its objections. The letter stated: "Oryana strongly urges that the proposed rule be withdrawn and resubmitted. The rule as proposed disregards many of the recommendations of the NOSB. It also disregards organic practices that have been institutionalized by decades of organic farmers. We urge that the rule be rewritten to comport with existing generally accepted practices of the organic farming community."

The USDA went back to the drawing board and after another problematic proposal followed by another comment period, issued a workable final rule in 2000. The farmers, consumer advocacy groups, and co-ops had spoken!

Oryana's mission states that providing high quality food produced in ecologically sound ways at fair value to owners and the community is top priority. It further states that Oryana owners and staff are committed to enhancing their community through the practice of cooperative economics and education about the relationship of food to health. In keeping true to this mission, Oryana sought to develop relationships with local organic farmers and prioritized organic products.

John and Julia Brabanec were one of the first farming couples to supply Oryana with a variety of organic produce beginning in the late 70s. In a 2000 Oryana newsletter article about the meaning of organic agriculture, John summed things up nicely when he stated, "Organic means safe and wholesome food both for us and for our customers, food that will foster robust health. Secondly, it means our farm is healthy, not only for the sake of the planet but also for our own health and safety as workers and all the living creatures who share that place with us."

In addition to forming relationships with local organic farmers, Oryana took an extraordinary step in demonstrating its long-standing commitment to the importance of organic food when it became the first Certified Organic co-op in the United States in 2002. Being a Certified Organic retailer does not mean that everything in the store is organic, but does mean that it provides a level of assurance to owners and customers that the integrity of the organic products are protected from farm to shopping cart. To be certified, Oryana must comply with strict USDA rules that include storewide and departmental procedures, staff trainings, a filtered water supply, proper storage and handling of organic foods, and a paper trail of third party certifications, to name just a few. Recertification is done on a yearly basis. The Grain Train in Petoskey also acquired Certified Organic retailer status in 2012.

The future of co-ops in Michigan

Like other co-ops in Michigan, Oryana faces increasing competition not only from large scale grocers and retailers that have incorporated organic foods into their product mix, but also the impending openings of Lucky's Market and Costco Wholesale Warehouse, both within five miles of the store. "By 2015, even the conventional grocers sold the highest percentage of natural and organic products," said Steve Nance, Oryana's general manager. Other natural foods store chains such as Whole Foods Market, Plum Market, Fresh Thyme Market, and Earth Fare have been sprouting up with increasing frequency throughout the state, in some cases within sight of a co-op. It took a few decades but our trailblazing food co-ops evidently got the message across that whole, organic foods are in everyone's best interest. "Michigan cooperatives had been successful in their mission to educate on the relationship of food and health and ecological sustainability," Steve said. "And people finally got it!"

For Oryana, the hope is that the emphasis on *organic* and *local* as well as *community* will continue to set it apart from the competition, in spite of competitors' claims to be "natural" and "organic." "The challenge for our co-op," according to Steve, "is one familiar to any business in a competitive environment, how to differentiate ourselves and remain viable and sustainable." As per the co-op buying guidelines, *organic* is still the top consideration of whether or not to carry a product in the store and *local* products must come from within 100 miles. Owners and shoppers of Oryana, although budget conscious, are also savvy, and Oryana believes they understand the co-op's commitment to community and organics and will remain faithful in the long run. "We still believe in organic as strongly as ever," said Sandi McArthur. "We have more local support than ever. Our commitment to organic is a testament to who we are and what we stand for."

Co-ops have always supported clean, local, and organic food and will remain vigilant in protecting the national organic standards in the face of the anti-health and anti-environment agenda of our current Congress. Oryana and co-ops worldwide operate by a set of principles designed by the Rochdale Pioneers, principles such as *education* and *concern for community* that translate into providing educational opportunities related to healthy food and food systems. Protecting the integrity of our food is critical to our health and the health of our planet and food co-ops will help ensure that the organic movement remains vital.

Luise Bolleber is the Outreach & Marketing Specialist at Oryana Community Cooperative and holds an MFA in creative non-fiction writing from Lesley University in Cambridge, Massachusetts. She is passionate about organic agriculture and is proud to work for a co-op business that places such a high priority on organic food.

beginningfarmers.org : An Internet Resource for Aspiring and Beginning Farmers in Michigan and Beyond

Taylor Reid

I am not a web designer or a computer guy. I am not even technologically savvy, really. But in the summer of 2008 I was spending a lot of time surfing the web. I was working on my Ph.D. at Michigan State University in the Department of Community, Agriculture, Recreation, and Resource Studies, and I had become very interested in beginning farmers. Specifically, my interest was in the emerging group of farmers who had somehow found their way into agriculture without farming backgrounds. And I was meeting a lot of these folks who were selling their products locally through CSAs, roadside stands, at farmers markets, and through local food co-ops. My dissertation project was focused on the learning processes that these farmers went through to get started. How would someone who was interested in farming figure out all of the many things they need to know to farm?

Trying to put myself in their shoes, I started asking, "If I wanted to farm, how would I figure out how to do it?" I could go out and intern with an established farmer, learn the trade in the old fashioned way of an apprentice, but there must be other ways as well. Being sequestered in the basement of an academic building at a large university, the first thing I asked myself, of course, was "what's on the internet?" And the answer surprised me.

Today if you type "how to start a farm" into a search engine, you will find a lot of websites (including www. beginningfarmers.org) that answer this query with step by step plans, and loads of links to useful resources. In 2008 that wasn't the case. There were resources out there on production, a few on financing, and some stuff on marketing, but they were scattered across many different websites, and were not organized in any way. I kept looking for the definitive resource and kept finding that it wasn't there. One day a lightbulb came on in my head: "Why don't I do that," I thought, "how hard could it be?"

So with this somewhat naïve and optimistic idea, I set to work. Well, it turned out to be harder than just filling out a couple of forms and sending in a check. And there were a couple of moments in the beginning when I was very close to simply throwing in the towel. What I found was that if I wanted to do it right (and why do it at all if I didn't), there was a technical learning curve that was pretty steep. Website design and management combines a whole set of skills—from graphic design, to information technology, to small business management—that I had none of. Finally I decided to hire someone to do the initial design and navigate me through the process of setting up a domain. It was the right decision, and in July of 2008 www.beginningfarmers.org was unceremoniously launched.

In hindsight, I started the website without any real idea of what I wanted to do with it, or what it might be. I just wanted to develop a resource that people could use to get started in farming. I chose the .org designation partly because beginningfarmers.com was already owned by someone, but partly because I thought that this effort could grow into something bigger someday. That's about as far as my vision went.

The first thing I did was to start compiling all of the disparate resources I had been finding on the internet. I made a production resources page, a marketing resources page, a finding land page, and a finding funding / grants page. The real revelation however, came when I started learning how to use the blog. The person I had hired to help me set up the website had strongly encouraged me to set it up as a blog site, and I had agreed, even though I had only the foggiest notion of what that was.

A blog is a regularly updated website that is constantly posting new stories, new material, new ideas, and new resources. And as I started putting together resources from around the internet, I began posting the content of the pages I was building to the blog. Much to my surprise, once I started doing this, people started visiting the site. At first it was just a couple of people every day or two, but that was thrilling enough. I had an audience! As I began to add regular content, the numbers started growing, and growing, and I was hooked.

I had no idea what I was doing really, I was just throwing content up on the web in the beginning, and I made some naïve mistakes that seem funny in retrospect. Somehow I had no intuitive sense that other internet content might be protected by copyright, so I shared whatever I found out there. It wasn't long before I got an e-mail from someone asking me to take their content off of my site. I was so embarrassed and apologetic that the person ended up helping me out with one of the first high profile links to my new website, and I am still thankful to the administrator of the wonderful home canning and preserving website pickyourown.org for doing that.

There was so much technical information to learn, and so little of it was intuitive to me, that administering the site was a real struggle a lot of the time. Website architecture is complex, and HTML code is like a foreign language. But the medium was so new, and so many people were starting the use the site, that I was motivated to learn. Eventually I developed a little bit of a community between the site and its corresponding Facebook page (another thing I was an accidental early adopter of). When beginningfarmers.org crashed unexpectedly in 2010, I found a hobby farmer with web development skills who was willing to help me out. So much of what I learned was by trial and error and through the generosity of strangers I stumbled into on the internet.

Over time I got better at generating regular content that people were interested in: event announcements, original articles, internship and job listings, profiles of beginning farmer organizations.... I was adding new blog posts almost every day to augment fixed pages on how to start a farm, where to find loans and grants, beginning farmer training programs, finding land to farm, production resources, marketing resources, and much, much more.

My biggest challenge was in monetization of the site. Here I was year after year spending 10 hours a week or more administering a website that lots of people were using, but I wasn't able to pay myself. Eventually I got a few small natural products companies to pay a little bit for sidebar ads, and used Google Adsense to augment that. It was enough to pay the hosting cost for the site and provide me with a little bit of money for my time, but certainly nothing even close to minimum wage.

Despite my commitment to providing an important resource for promoting sustainable farming, small farms, and beginning farmer entry, by 2012 the website was starting to be a drain. My wife and I were expecting a baby, and I was trying to make the final push to finish my dissertation at MSU. That spring I got a purchase offer from a company called AgHub (now Carbon Media Group) that provided me with an exit strategy. The buyout we negotiated in the summer of 2012 compensated me for some of the work I had done to build the site, and took the onerous and tedious job of technical administration and monetization off my hands. Since that time I have continued to work for the site as a contractor, developing content and providing regular web posts.

From the beginning, the content on the site has reflected my own vision of sustainable farming systems. It has always been geared primarily toward building small scale, organic, and community based farming enterprises. This has gained the site a loyal following, but has probably limited its appeal in some ways as well. While I have also tried to generate content that is useful for someone in Alabama who wants to start a contract chicken farm, or someone in Nebraska who wants to take over a 1000 acre field crop operation, this isn't really my area of expertise, and I have chosen to write mainly about what I know well.

Today beginningfarmers.org gets more than 50,000 visitors each month, and has 16,000 Facebook followers. I still enjoy finding information and doing the posts, and it is gratifying to know that they reach so many people. This project has also allowed me to meet a lot of amazing people, taken me to exciting events like Growing Power and Farm Aid, and was really my gateway into sustainable agriculture activism and policy work. My greatest hope, however, is that beginningfarmers.org continues to provide a valuable resource for helping aspiring farmers to find their way into agriculture.

Taylor Reid holds degrees in Plant and Soil Science (B.S., University of Massachusetts), Botany and Plant Pathology (M.S., Michigan State University), and Community, Food, and Agriculture (Ph.D., Michigan State University). He is currently the Sustainable Farming and Food Systems Program Chair, and Farm Education Director, at Tompkins Cortland Community College in Dryden, New York. His research has focused on the values, motivations, and learning processes of first-generation farmers, and on the organic farming movement in Michigan. He is a former Chair of the Michigan Integrated Food and Farming Systems (MIFFS) Ag. Policy Committee, and served on the Michigan Organic Food and Farm Alliance (MOFFA) Board of Directors from 2006-2009.

Organic Soil Management

Joe Scrimger

Introduction

To begin this discussion on Organic Soil Management, first some history will be given about how I came to look for a process of 'Soil Balance'. Second, some technical points will be covered in the soil balancing process in order to create the type of dynamics needed to achieve proper nutrition. Third, a table of target soil test levels will be given as a guide. This guide explains the two types of tests used for the base part of the testing system. Fourth, additional reading will be noted for those who desire to know more about the soil processes.

It should also be said that there are a lot of good approaches to Organic Soil Management, what is discussed here is a process that has worked for us. To get to where we are we had to be open to different approaches and we think that you should be open also.

History

My wife Kay and I purchased a 160 acre farm in the fall of 1972. At the time, I was selling farm equipment for a local dealer and doing custom harvesting. Our plan was to farm the land conventionally, but after some real life lessons on the fluctuation of the commodity market and dealing with personal health issues, we decided to look for something different. At the same time my father, who had been a dairy farmer, was dying from colon cancer. I had this intuition that his condition may be more about food and agriculture than I knew. I was fortunate to have in-laws that were farming their 50 cow dairy organically, and

I noticed that their crop production appeared to affect the health of the cows more positively than the conventional crop production I had grown up with.

During this time I also became active with the American Agriculture Movement (AAM) in the region. We discussed the farm pricing system in United States agriculture and learned about 'Parity' or the balance that was lacking in the pricing of food in our system. I soon concluded that 'Parity', or balance, starts in the soil and not at the local grain elevator or at the USDA in Washington DC.

I spent 20 years pursuing that balance. Added to that, another 20 years of working with other farmers sharing what I had learned through a soil testing and contract consulting business call Bio-Systems. My business had not only allowed me to share the knowledge that I had gained, but it also allowed me to learn from some of the best farmers in the Midwest. I now feel it is important to share this history because I came about managing the soil organically in an 'organic' way. My formal education was in mechanical engineering but my real education has been continuously learning about our food systems from the soil up and how we can use our food system much more to our physical and financial benefit, than is promoted in the conventional agricultural world.

The Rules

There are a couple of principles that I follow when it comes to managing the soil. The first is that 'Mother Nature' will limit the yield to balance the minerals in the production and that if we supply the needed minerals we are not limited in production. This explains why some organic farmers get less yield in some area in the transition, but it also sets the stage that if we supply the minerals, yield is not limited. The second principle comes from one of my teachers who stressed that all degenerative diseases are caused by mineral deficiencies. Over the years I have found this to be very true.

The biology that affects mineral release in the soil also needs to be considered. Organic farmers certainly focus on building organic matter and organic matter does affect soil biology positively. Some schools of thought like to focus more on biology whereas some focus more on minerals. What I see is that the two work very complementary to each other. It doesn't matter which came first or is more important, they are both needed for farms to be successful. Therefore we should try not to get caught in the debate.

Physical Signs

One way of measuring the amount of biology in the soil is by looking at some physical evidence. First, we can smell the soil. It should have that musty/woodsy smell that the actinomycete bacteria give off in a good, biologically active soil. This perhaps is one of the first soil tests to be performed. I noticed that this basic smell was missing in many conventional farms by the late 1970s and 80s. Along with the smell, they also lost their earthworms. Most of these farms were applying more fertilizer in the N-P-K conventional water soluble, salt based form that was hurting the beneficial biology in the soil. At the time, most farmers were not being told about the beneficial soil biology, but about the detrimental parts and how to fight them. Because of this discussion, the agriculture of the time lost the dynamics between the minerals and biology that are important to the efficiency and health of the soil.

Chemical Effects

Organic field crop and dairy farms did not have much pest or disease pressure in the early 70s and 80s. However, as I spent more time with 'Conventional' fruit and vegetable growers across Michigan and Southwest Ontario I began to see that pesticides were being applied in the amount of $500 per acre to intensive fruit operations and $100 to $200 per acre being applied to vegetable crops. This too was affecting the dynamic relationship between the beneficial biology and minerals in the soil because the pesticides had eliminated the beneficial communities along with the detrimental ones.

I mention this because there is another rule provided by 'Mother Nature' that I noticed. It is that when overall biology in the soil decreases, the unbeneficial organisms always increase. The reverse in also true, when the overall biology in the soil increases there is a corresponding decrease in detrimental organisms. This explains some of what I saw in the first organic farms I visited. They had less pest pressure naturally. They had more overall soil biology resulting in less disease. I don't think I would have been taught any of this in an Ag College in the late 1960s and early 1970s.

Learning to Build Soil

I have watched organic farmers intensively use cover crops, deep rooting legumes, green manure and crop rotation to build their soil. I have used these methods on my own farm as well. This can work but it can also depend on how much soil mineral reserves the farm had to start with and how the mineral reserves were balanced. We also have to consider at what point their soil really started to function dynamically to build and maintain their overall fertility that would help determine the long term success of the farm.

Considerations

Back to that balance factor and supplying the needed mineral for production, nitrogen and potash are a couple of minerals that do relate to yield, but need to be controlled in the short term for long term balance. Both nutrients can lead to luxury feeding or over feeding the plant, limiting other mineral uptake and creating mineral deficiencies. Remember all degenerative diseases are caused by mineral deficiencies. Most of the ag industry in the past knew of nitrate poisoning from corn receiving too much nitrogen in drought conditions. In addition, dairy farmers understand about problems of too much potassium in the hay that caused breeding and many other problems in the barn. But most farmers today are disconnected from the direct visual tie to animal health on their farm because of the consolidation of confinement animal feeding operations. Excesses are hard to balance in feeding systems, so the balance needs to come from the soil. Balance is needed to achieve proper cell structure in the plant at all stages of growth; it is also needed for the plant to be more pest and disease resistant during those stages. This is a major point to which conventional agriculture really does not pay attention.

In the 20 years of pursuing balance, I was able to experiment on my organic farm. I was able to play with different approaches to achieving balance, including surface tillage compared to moldboard plowing. Initially I used an expensive 2-way rollover moldboard plow that over time did not enhance the decay process and led to deeper compacted layers in the soil. When I switched to surface tillage methods, such as chisel plowing, disking and field cultivating I could see crop residue would break down much faster and water movement into the soil improve. I also experimented on whether adding minerals to the soil really made a difference. I had a field that had not had any off-farm inputs for over 25 years. In some fields, I applied colloidal phosphate for beans, others got an organic fertilizer blend for corn, and some got cattle manure in the rotation for corn and hay. I also employed the use of green manure, deep rooting legumes, and cover crops. Since our phosphate reserves were low on the farm, the areas that received the colloidal phosphate responded the most in yield and quality. Today the farm receives a readily available mix of compost and colloidal phosphate and/or gypsum (calcium sulfate) along with any trace minerals as needed to build the soil levels for more optimal plant nutrition and production. In the first years of organic farming the focus was more on controlling costs, whereas today's market justifies the cost of soil building with keeping the idea of quality, nutrient density and yield in mind. During the first years, I could see the soil had the needed biology but the minerals were low. I added minerals to this soil, as the budget would allow, and I could see the dynamics of the minerals and biology working together.

So having said these things, I am going to move on to some of the technical aspects of balancing soils on a biological and mineral basis. Please keep in mind that the soil wants to work and you don't have to know all the science behind its function. However, in our economy we do have to have efficiency to stay in the farming business. Understanding how the soil functions can greatly help the efficiency of the farm. And, believe it or not, there once was a time I thought there was no correlation between soil tests and yield outcome. This premature conclusion came before I had tested the minerals in many organic and conventional farms. Once I factored in how the 'biology' affects the minerals, with a test that checked the solubility of the base nutrients and gave an affordable, indirect measurement of the biology, I could see the need for testing.

Managing Soil Organically – The Technical Side

Managing soil organically with crop rotation, green manures, cover crops, animal manure/compost, and rock minerals can and has worked very well for many 'organic' farms, but what we are going to discuss here is managing soils for proper nutrient density in the production, and the technology that is available today to track this process. This is a system that produces nutritionally balanced crops that are more pest and disease resistant while being better feed for animals and food for people. It is based on building a soil system as opposed to creating a fertilizer system. The soil amendments used in an organic system tend to be organic matter or rock mineral based. Therefore, there needs to be consideration not only that the balance is different but also that the soil amendments release differently than those in a conventional fertilizer. It is the balance of beneficial soil organisms, like nitrogen fixing bacteria and mycorrhizal fungi, which break down these amendments to allow them to be available to the plant. For that reason, achieving a balance of beneficial soil bacteria and fungi, while providing the necessary minerals, becomes essential to managing soil organically. It is also essential to understand the soil system we are talking about here does not include the extreme of low land, muck soils, or recommendations for blueberries, which can be farmed organically, but need a different balancing system than the high ground, mineral soils, and crops we are covering.

Organic Matter

The most sensible place to start is a discussion of organic matter, which historically most organic farmers have a keen focus on. Organic matter serves as a source of energy for soil microorganisms and as a source of plant nutrients. It holds the minerals absorbed from the soil against loss by leaching until they are released by the actions of microorganisms. Bacteria thriving on the organic matter produce complex carbohydrates that provide the glue that holds the soil particles together as aggregates. Acids produced in the decomposition of organic matter can make soil mineral reserves, or rock minerals added to the soil, available to the plant. Penetration of roots through the soil is improved by good structure brought about by the decomposition of organic matter. With soil managed organically there needs to be a focus on building organic

matter and using practices that will decrease soil compaction, such as green manure, manure, or compost along
with crop rotations and deep rooting legumes. Depending
on the state of the soil and the intensity of the soil building
practices, the soil biology will start to improve in the first
couple of years on conventional farmed soil in transition to
organics and can become active in 3-5 years. Proper balance of the biology and minerals may take 7-10 years to
accomplish, after which it is very easy to maintain.

Nitrogen

Organic matter can make the natural nitrogen cycle
work. However, if it falls below a level required to free
enough nitrogen from microorganisms an additional source
of organic nitrogen may be needed. A properly working soil
at three percent organic matter should release close to 100
pounds of nitrogen over the course of the year, before the
manure, compost or legumes are factored in. Therefore
managing nitrogen becomes essential, because it can be
easy to have too much, although a lot of farms are still
applying more. The proper amount of nitrogen helps build
good cell structure in the plant and decreases fungal
disease pressure when balanced with other nutrients. Too
much nitrogen can lead to increased fungal disease and
pest invasion, because it restricts other mineral uptake and
in turn decreases plant cell structure quality. It can also
lead to leaching and soil compaction, even with organic
nitrogen sources. Too little soil nitrogen will decrease yield
potential. So you can see that nitrogen can be a very
limiting factor in the transition that needs to be addressed
early on, and monitored through soil testing, to see when
the dynamics of the soil bacteria kick in so you don't end up
with too much, which can be as harmful to the farm as not
having enough.

Calcium

Nitrogen is a very important nutrient to have working in an organic soil system, but most likely we would have had to address the basics of pH and calcium levels to start to have some efficiency with nitrogen management and use. The soil's inability to produce nitrogen and lack of soluble calcium indicates a lack of beneficial soil bacteria. Regardless of the type of soil or where the farm is in the transition, applying calcium does encourage soil bacteria, as long as you are applying other organic matter sources such as manure, green manure, or compost with the calcium. Calcium carries the most value in an organic system because it tends to relate to most other nutrient release; for that reason 70-75% base saturation of calcium is desired for most vegetable or fruit crops, along with a 6.5 to 6.7 – slightly acid – pH level.

Potash

Potassium is also a very important plant nutrient, but needs to be closely monitored, especially in the transition. Some of what it is responsible for is the set and size of the seed, cellulose production, and improving drought resistance. However, it is one of the two most misused nutrients, nitrogen being the other. In organic agriculture, it does not take as much potash to build or maintain adequate levels because potash is one of the easiest nutrients to get soluble in good working soil. It is easy to recycle with crop residue management or mulching. For soils with high holding capacity, like a clay or high organic matter soil, 2-3% potash base saturation may be enough. If the soil has a low holding capacity, like sand, 3-4% potash base saturation may be needed. One error that some farmers make is that they don't take the potassium in manure, compost, green manures, or recycled crop residues into account. It may be evident on a soil test that potassium is needed, but you need to consider all the practices that are being used before calculating the amount of potash to apply.

Sulfur

When managing soil organically, sulfur tends to be very important when you are working with extra nitrogen, which most organic farms are over time. It should be considered a major element along with phosphate and potash. Many legume crops, such as beans or alfalfa, can use more sulfates than phosphates, especially after the soil starts to produce nitrogen. Among its many roles, sulfur plays an important part in protein formation. There is an intricate relationship between sulfur and its effect on nitrate accumulation, crude protein levels, and the biological value of plant proteins. When sulfur is low, the nitrates accumulate in the plant tissue instead of forming into amino acids and protein. Adding sulfur will help slow down nitrogen release. It does this by how it feeds the microbes, like the actinomycetes, that are processing the nitrogen. It makes more complete proteins in their bodies, which in turn will come back as slow release nitrogen and increases in soil organic matter in the longer term. Most soil tests that I have come across are less than 10 ppm on a base test. For optimal function and overall balance, a 30 to 40 ppm is desired, which should be built up over time as your soil nitrogen production potential improves.

Trace Elements

Trace elements need to be looked at as part of the process that gives your soil more minerals to pass on to the plant. A boron application will help the plant metabolize calcium, whereas zinc will help metabolize phosphate. Sometimes the trace elements won't make a yield difference, in the short term, but rather a quality difference that shows over time. This quality may be reflected in pest and disease resistance, better recovery from stress, more flavor in the crop, or better vitality in the seed and feed. The microbes in the soil also need trace elements to make complete protein in their bodies, which in turn compliment the protein production in the plant, and is passed on to the animal. Where trace elements are low, a kelp and chelated trace element solution can be used as a foliar and is an efficient short term approach for the plant, that many organic growers use, but deficiencies in the soil should and will need to be addressed to achieve proper soil dynamics.

Phosphate

In the Great Lakes Region, a lot of the soil phosphate tends to be tied up and is building up in the soil, not being released to the plant. This shows up on many farms where the organic matter is decreasing, or where anaerobic liquid manure is being used. Soil phosphate solubility is regulated by beneficial soil organisms, such as mycorrhizal fungi, and can be measured directly. This is where a water soluble test, such as a Bio-Test, can come into play. Most base tests will report adequate phosphate or phosphorus levels and no recommendations will be made to amend the soil. However, on a soluble test, phosphate levels are much less than adequate. The only way to get phosphate to release from the soil and become available to the plant is for the fungal organism to digest it. Most Michigan soils tend to be bacterial dominated, which is another factor in the soil phosphate build up, lack of quality in production, and environmental impacts in the Great Lakes. If a base test reports higher levels of phosphate than the water soluble test, we know the soil is lacking the much needed fungal organisms. In an organic system, adding amendments is not always about replacing deficiencies, it is also about supplying the minerals needed to make the plant and the soil function at its best. If your phosphate was low, below 22 ppm phosphorus on a base CEC test, it will need to be addressed early because most phosphate amendments are slow release and will take time to be weathered and digested by the soil. Soil bacterial and fungal organisms may not be at adequate levels in the transition to digest the mineral forms of phosphate; consequently, a more soluble form such as bone meal or poultry compost may be needed. Keep in mind poultry compost shouldn't be over-used because of how it affects the nitrogen cycle. In addition, bone meal can be very costly, and one needs to be sure it is allowed through their certifier. Colloidal phosphate, soft rock phosphate, as well as brown and black rock phosphates, are all typical mineral sources of phosphate that have been used in organic systems.

In the same way that nitrogen is a two part process of adding nitrogen sources to the soil and getting beneficial soil bacteria to produce nitrogen, phosphate is also a two part process of building the soil levels and getting the beneficial soil fungal organisms to digest it. If the soils have been depleted of organic matter or phosphate reserves, this may take 5-10 years or longer. The bacterial process for nitrogen production can be built relatively quickly and needs to be first and then managed while the soil fungal organisms are fed higher carbon materials. Examples of high carbon materials are high carbon compost and mature crop residues, versus just green cover crops or legumes that primarily feed the bacteria. In organic production, phosphate tends to be slow release, especially in colder northern climates, and it may take over 45 ppm of reserve phosphate to come up with adequate soluble phosphate to support fast, nutritional growth in cooler conditions. This is why successful organic farmers of the past used to apply a ton per acre of rock phosphate that may have lasted them 10 years or more. These farmers did not have the same phosphate runoff problems that we see in the Great Lakes Region today. Soils that have adequate organic matter and healthy fungal communities are less susceptible to erosion, so there is less chance of phosphate runoff into the environment.

Weeds Are Indicators

Quackgrass

We can't discuss organic soil management without talking about weeds. There once was a time when a field could be plowed and planted and weeds were not always the first to grow. We did not get to this point of excess weeds overnight. However, there are some basic steps that can be taken to help manage weed pressure. Quackgrass, lambsquarters, and pigweed are classic weeds that we will touch on. Quackgrass pressure usually indicates a lack of soluble calcium and a lack of decay, that is the responsibility of the soil microbes. Most of conventional agriculture doesn't have enough soil beneficial microbes, and quackgrass was primarily why conventional agriculture came out with atrazine and glyphosate (Roundup) herbicides, which became the norm in the 1970s. Using these herbicides affects decay because they are detrimental to the soil microbes. Consequently, herbicide use reduces the soluble calcium, which creates more quackgrass pressure. This is great if you are selling the herbicides but not so good if you are buying them. Because calcium is needed in most plants for basic proper cell structure and in the soil for other nutrient function, you can see that the process of using herbicides isn't beneficial for many reasons. As many experienced organic farmers have found, surface tillage or mulching done properly will reduce overall quackgrass pressure and enhance decay.

Lambsquarters and Pigweed

Lambsquarters and pigweed, on the other hand, tend to be indicators of good soil. Both indicate rich fertile soil but lambsquarters also indicates good decay of organic matter and high humus. The problem comes when they become hard to control. This usually indicates excess nutrients in the way of nitrogen and/or potash. Because the plants and weeds live off of the soluble nutrients and potash is easy to make soluble, it is usually where the imbalance lies, especially when you are trying to build the soil. As you achieve better phosphate solubility, you do not need as much nitrogen or potash because of the soil dynamics that you are accumulating. Timely cultivation, cover cropping, and composting will all help control these broadleaf weeds as the system balances.

Not all weeds and pests can be explained by a soil test. As plant diversity in the community has changed through breeding, monocultures and large consolidated farms have all affected how we manage pests organically. Balancing minerals is just one part of this process and the biology is another. It also will take ecological balance in the soil and diversity to attain the full dynamics of natural pest control.

Concluding Thoughts

An organic system is more than just not applying conventional amendments to the soil. If we use what is known about beneficial soil biology and how organic amendments work, while utilizing both reserve and water soluble soil tests, we can achieve the balance that I searched for. With this, we can provide what the public needs—a system of food production that is environmentally sound and economically viable, producing food that can rebuild and sustain the wealth and health of a nation. This can be done in a way that is actually more productive than the conventional agricultural model of the last 60 years. Let's work together as farmers and consumers to get this organic process growing.

BIO-SYSTEMS' GUIDE TO SOIL TESTING

Types of Soil Tests

We have two types of soil tests available. The first type, called the CATION EXCHANGE CAPACITY or C.E.C. test, measures the total of each nutrient present in the soil. This includes both available and extractable reserve nutrients. The second type, the BIO-TEST, measures only the amount of nutrients available to the plant at that time and conditions of the test. The BIO-TEST should be performed during the growing season.

Why Two Soil Tests?

The results of both the tests allow us to compare the current fertility of the soil with its potential fertility and give us an idea of the amount of biological activity present. This helps us to give a more complete recommendation. Nitrate and calcium solubility on the BIO-TEST indicates soil bacterial activity. The phosphate solubility on the BIO-TEST compared to the base C.E.C. TEST reading can indicate beneficial soil fungal organisms

When Should I Test?

BIO-TESTS should be taken periodically throughout the season to determine pre-plant fertilizer and lime, mid-season sidedress and fall base fertilizer and lime needs. C.E.C. TESTS can be taken whenever convenient and should be useful for 1-3 years, depending on the type of soil building program used.

The chart below lists our desired (target) ranges for the items tested on each type of soil test. Nutrients are expressed in pounds per acre (#/A) unless otherwise noted.

	C.E.C. TEST	BIO-TEST
Organic Matter	3-5%	
Nitrate		50-70 (Grain Crops)
Ammonia		<10
Available P2O5		120-200
P1 (Phosphate)	200-400	
P2 (Phosphate)	400+	
Soluble K2O		120-140
K2O (Potash)	200-400	
Magnesium	200-400	
Soluble Calcium		2000-5600+
Calcium	3000+	
pH Soil	6.5-6.8	6.5-6.8
C.E.C.	10+	
Energy (ergs)		200-600
% Base Sat K	2-4%	
% Base Sat Mg	12-13%	
% Base Sat CA	75-80%	
% Base Sat H	3-5%	
Sulphur	18-35 ppm	
Zinc	5-8 ppm	
Manganese	22-45 ppm	
Iron	25-50 ppm	
Copper	2-3 ppm	
Boron	2.5-3 ppm	

Some further reading is listed below:

Eco-Farm, An Acres USA Primer by Charles Waters discusses soil fertility, animal health, weeds as indicators, etc.

From the Soil Up by Donald L. Schriefer discusses tillage, soil dynamics, fertility, aeration, moisture management and residue decay, not an organic book but a book explaining the principles of fertility.

Field Crop Ecology, MSU Extension Bulletin E-2646, discusses field crop ecology and soil ecology that includes some of the biotic soil components, carbon, nitrogen, cover crops, pest ecology and management, insect community and nematodes.

Electrolytes, the Spark of Life by Gillian Martlew N.D., an explanation of the importance of trace minerals.

Soil Biology Primer by the Soil and Water Conservation Society, basics of the Soil Food Web.

Books by Dan Skow D.V.M. or Arden Anderson on the teachings of Dr. Carey Reams.

Joe and Kay Scrimger started Organic farming in 1973 and by 1975 transitioned 280 acres to an organic program. Scrimger Farm now has 130 acres and is certified by OCIA. Joe is currently the interim president of the Farm to Consumer Foundation, of which he has been a board member since 2012. He was a founding member and first Chairman of Michigan Thumb Organics (MTO) from 1999-2012. From 1976-2002 he was an OGM member, Thumb Chair and State Chair along with other positions. He also was a founding member and first chairman of Organic Farmers of Michigan (OFM) in 1993-1999. Joe currently owns and manages Bio-Systems, an independent soil testing and consulting business he started in 1980 in Marlette, MI.

PART IV: Organic Farming, Now More Important Than Ever

Organics—The New Industry

Jessie and Leah Smith

It is generally accepted that big business controls a great deal of money. However, as the power of a few massive companies continues to grow unchallenged by competition, unlimited by government regulations, and apparently unfettered by ethics, their control has extended over more than just money. It is control over a basic human need, food, and reaches all the way from soil to citizen.

The mechanisms that have brought this about are described thoroughly in the 2016 book by Philip H. Howard, *Concentration and Power in the Food System: Who Controls What We Eat?*.[1] An associate professor at Michigan State University, Howard has gained a reputation for exposing the true nature of the food industry with the creation of (and wide appreciation for) his numerous "bubble" charts. These charts have covered several topics, including top U.S. beer firms, seed industry acquisitions, and alliances and organic food brand acquisitions. According to Howard, part of the motivation for the creation of these bubble charts was the hidden nature of buyouts in the organic food industry.[2]

---

[1] Howard, Philip H. 2016. *Concentration and Power in the Food System: Who Controls What We Eat?*. New York, NY: Bloomsbury Publishing Plc.

[2] Walters, Chris. 2016. "Interview: Food System Consolidation: Professor, Author Philip Howard Discusses Corporate Control of Organic Brands, Profits." *Acres USA,* Vol. 46, No. 8: 54-64.

We are grateful to him for both his well researched work about the current organic food industry, and for the hopeful words he offers for the future.

The passage of the Organic Foods Production Act of 1990 and the resulting USDA National Organic Standards (NOS) signaled a change in organic agriculture. Obviously, interest in this segment of agriculture had increased on the part of the consumer. Greater consumer interest is bound to attract the big business capitalists who are ready to make more money. And they are now involved in every level of the organic food system, specifically retail, processing, distribution and production, and agricultural inputs.

The lack of nationalized organic standards had been a major stumbling block to the entrance of big business into organic agriculture. How can you process organic products and ship them to distant locations if there is the possibility they will not conform with the regional organic standards where they are sent? This is why there was significant interest in and involvement with the writing of the national organic standards on the part of big business.

The initial draft of the organic standards seemed hardly worth the name, and the hand of big business interests was clearly visible. For example, the standards as published in 1997 allowed the use of genetic engineering, sewage sludge, and irradiation (the Big Three) in what was to be certified as organic. None of the three had ever had a place in organic agriculture prior to this and they were obviously suggested to make subsequent proposals for the inclusion of doubtful practices appear less unreasonable. The resulting public outcry led to changes, including the removal of the Big Three as acceptable practices, and an improved set of standards was put into place in 2002. Still, though the standards were an improvement from the initial draft, many "veterans" of the organic movement felt that the soul had been taken out of organic agriculture. And with this standardization, as expected, came the big business interests who could now enter into a whole new market, and the increase in the market shares of large companies has been rapid.

The people who participated in the growth of the organic movement beginning in the 1970s were not interested in the food produced by large corporations. That is why they struck out on their own to create a means of distributing and selling the kind of foods they wanted, in both cases on a comparatively small scale. Small, but numerous. In the 1970s, more than 5,000 food buying co-ops were founded to provide alternatives to conventional agriculture's branded items. These stores were supplied by small, largely cooperatively owned companies who were in the business of distributing natural foods. Needless to say, there was no such thing as organics in any ordinary grocery store at the time.

The recent involvement of big business in the organic retail and distribution arenas has led to high levels of concentration for both. Concentration is a term that describes the breadth of a given market: unconcentrated, freely competitive, and involving many companies at one end of the scale and concentrated, with little competition and the involvement of a few very large companies, at the other end.

The distribution of natural foods is now so concentrated that two distributors control 80% of the market, with the publicly traded gargantuan United Natural Foods Incorporated (UNFI) being at the top.[3] The reduction in the number of companies involved in distribution has come about not by

---

[3] Sligh, Michael, and Carolyn Christman. 2003. *Who Owns Organic? The Global Status, Prospects, and Challenges of a Changing Organic Market.* Pittsboro, NC: Rural Advancement Foundation International-USA.

small competition being pushed out but by it being bought up. The result is still a near monopoly and a lack of choice as well as power on the part of the consumer.

The retail picture is much the same, though the change has come about somewhat differently. While there were once 5,000 food buying co-ops, the number has dwindled to 300, with most of them simply ceasing to exist. On the other hand, the health food stores Whole Foods and Wild Oats have bought out competitors, become publicly traded, and eventually combined with each other, in 2007, to become the new Whole Foods, bigger than ever. Both UNFI and Whole Foods, each now in the hands of big business, hold extreme power in the natural foods industry and can exert major control over whether an organic brand makes it to the market or not.[4]

Organics have also moved beyond the specialized health foods stores and into the mainstream, with organic products now being available at stores like Walmart and Kroger. Though this is a clear indicator of big business involvement in organics, other changes have been more opaque. General Mills offers an excellent example. With suitable fanfare, it bought out LaraBar, Cascadian Farm, and Muir Glen in past decades. However, the buyout of Immaculate Baking passed without notice; no fanfare was wanted. Furthermore, the products of none of these four lines display the familiar General Mills "G."

Both underreported buyouts and the rather atypical lack-of-branding on the labeling of certain big business-owned products are forms of stealth ownership, a practice now common among big business interests with regard to the organic brands they own.[5] By not disclosing when organic brands are bought out, the new owners are hoping

---

[4] Howard, op. cit.

[5] Ibid.

to keep the customers originally attracted to a brand that previously represented the smaller scale agriculture and competitive business world they wished to support.

Cost-cutting and profit-boosting frequently top the list when a large company buys a smaller one, leading to a fundamental change in the processing and thus the end product the company is producing. Changing from domestically based sources to foreign raw materials, switching from certified organic to the vaguely defined "natural" supply, or the addition of cheaply obtained ultra-processed and artificial ingredients are a few of the strategies used. Customers are presented with a new end product that, though outwardly identical or very similar to the previous product, lacks authenticity on many levels. As the original buyouts may not have been publicized, the consumers were not even aware of the fact that they should have been keeping their eyes peeled for changes. For example, Dean Foods' acquisition of WhiteWave was followed by the switch from organic to natural soybean sources. As this switch was not announced, even the retailers failed to notice the change or make the necessary changes in their advertising.[6]

The actual act of farming has not become concentrated into the hands of big business as rapidly as other sectors of the food system. It remains a very uncertain business that isn't quite as appealing to the capitalists. Still, there has been change. Organic dairy production is one sector that has undergone significant change. Horizon and Aurora are two pioneers in the field who were bought out and whose practices have changed as a result. Herd sizes increased and it has been reported that access to outdoor grazing has become less of a guarantee. The Cornucopia Institute has

---

[6] Shlacter, Barry. 2009. "Grocers Irked to Find out Soymilk Non-organic." Fort Worth Star-Telegram, November 8. https://www.cornucopia.org/2009/11/grocers-irked-over-not-being-told-that-best-selling-soy-milk-is-no-longer-organic/.

recently called upon the Department of Justice and the Federal Trade Commission to enforce antitrust laws against The Dannon Company, which is seeking to buy WhiteWave in a move to concentrate the industry further.[7] The Cornucopia Institute is a family-scale farmer economic justice group and watchdog for the organic industry. With an eye to what is happening at the national level and in the various groups that have a voice in organics, Cornucopia works to strengthen the integrity of the organic label with action alerts, articles, and scorecards for consumers.

As on the other levels of the food industry, larger farming operations benefit not only from natural advantages that come with their large size but also from a host of engineered advantages via the government. These enable the large operations to offer a product to their customers more cheaply while at the same time making more profit than their smaller competitors. Advantages come in the form of direct farm subsidies; regulations that increase barriers for competitors; the government purchasing of excess product; subsidies for the purchasing of fertilizers, fuel, irrigation, and crop insurance; the government funding of technological advancements that will solely benefit farming on a large scale; and allowing large operations to maintain a severely underpaid workforce that must itself partake of public subsidies (food assistance, health care, housing, etc.) for its survival.

Big business has also shown interest in the area of agricultural inputs. An input of particular interest in recent years has been seeds—what you might call the key agricultural input. In the mid-1900s, there existed thousands of companies in the seed industry. Many were small and family-owned. The passage of the Plant Variety

---

[7] The Cornucopia Institute. 2016. "Don't Let Giant Corporations and Factory Farms Take Over the Organic Milk Business." https://www.cornucopia.org/danone2016/.

Protection Act (PVPA) of 1970 granted property rights protection for sexually reproducing seeds to business interests. Though it included exemptions for researchers and farmers, intrusions have gotten further and further into the once untouched arena of patenting living organisms since then; business has gotten bigger and pushed even harder. DuPont and Monsanto participated in the meetings that worked to successfully extend the scope of intellectual property protections.[8]

As the seed business looked more and more promising, chemical and commodities firms began to buy up the small, independent seed companies. At first, these chemical/seed companies' genetically engineered seeds were their primary interest for protection and sales, especially when they could sell their seed in a package deal with their chemical product, as illustrated by the various Roundup Ready/ Roundup duos.

Now these companies are easily moving beyond genetically engineered seeds and into traditionally bred hybrids, as their control over the seed industry has expanded to the extent that it allows this sort of control. This control over the seed industry has led to an increase in seed prices, naturally. Far worse, these profit-driven companies have "bought the right" to decide which seeds (i.e., which genetic traits) will be preserved for the future and which will not. For example, Seminis ceased to offer more than one-third of its entire stock of seed varieties (approximately 2,500 fruits and vegetables) in a step it called a cost saving measure prior to being bought by Monsanto.[9]

---

[8] Sell, Susan K. 2003. *Private Power, Public Law: The Globalization of Intellectual Property Rights*. Boston, MA: Cambridge University Press.

[9] Dillon, Matthew. 2005. "Monsanto Buys Seminis." New Farm, February 22. http://newfarm.rodaleinstitute.org/features/2005/0205/seminisbuy/.

Government-enforced intellectual property protections have not only benefited the chemical/seed industry, but have aided animal genetics firms as well. The control of animal genetics for a number of livestock species is extremely concentrated, so their influence is overpowering. The Erich Wesjohann (EW) Group and Hendrix Genetics are two companies which control upwards of 90% of various poultry markets in terms of sales.[10] Swine are also highly controlled in terms of sales and breeds. For big operations, the more streamlined and simplified it can be, and thus in term of animals the fewer breeds (meaning lack of variation) involved, the happier they are.

Yet again, government is being effectively used to reinforce and advance the advantage of big business and its ideals. For example, in 2011 the Department of Natural Resources in Michigan issued regulations that essentially outlawed heritage swine in the state on the basis of physical characteristics with no genetic criteria, claiming that control of these breeds was necessary to control the potential of feral pigs. Heritage swine farmers were ordered to kill their fenced livestock in a move that was strongly supported by the Michigan Pork Producers Association and the big business interests they represent. Lastly, with a cancer-esque desire for endless growth characteristic of these businesses, there is currently interest in expanding into the fish industry.

What effects do all of these changes, this concentration of business and power, have on the environment in which we live and will live in the future? We have already lost numerous varieties of edible plants, leaving us more vulnerable to climate change, diseases and pests that could drastically impact food crops. Plant genetics that could

---

[10] ETC Group. 2013. "Putting the Cartel Before the Horse ... and Farm, Seeds, Soil, Peasants, Etc." Communique No. 111. Ottawa, ON, Canada.

have helped to weather these conditions have been discarded and neglected in favor of those that produce in highly pampered and chemically enhanced conditions. Animal genetics have also been lost with the neglect of breeds that thrive on pasture or are hardy enough to weather less climate-controlled conditions in favor of animals that maintain high production levels with manufactured feed and antibiotics to keep them healthy in confined conditions.

This type of food system also leads to greater use of and dependence on fossil fuels (and greater attendant pollution) in terms of food transportation alone. Larger but fewer processing plants and distribution centers means longer trips both ways for the farthest reaching areas. A study published in 2001, comparing local/regionally based and conventional/nationally based food systems in Iowa, already showed a 4 to 17 times increase in fuel consumption and a near equivalent increase in CO_2 production.[11]

The state of California, despite producing many agricultural crops, also imports foods. The transportation of foods from out of state was shown to result in 45 times the amount of air pollution as compared to local or regional transportation of locally grown foods.[12] And naturally, replacing formerly locally sourced raw materials with cheaper, foreign sources (as was the case with WhiteWave's switch in soybean supply) will mean a great deal more fuel

---

[11] Pirog, Rich S.; Van Pelt, Timothy; Enshayan, Kamyar; and Cook, Ellen, "Food, Fuel, and Freeways: An Iowa perspective on how far food travels, fuel usage, and greenhouse gas emissions" (2001). Leopold Center Pubs and Papers. Paper 3. http://lib.dr.iastate.edu/leopold_pubspapers/3.

[12] Natural Resources Defense Council. 2007. "Food Miles: How far your food travels has serious consequences for your health and the climate." https://food-hub.org/files/resources/Food%20Miles.pdf.

consumed in travel yet again, and that much more pollution produced.

It remains true that organic farming systems do not use the chemical fertilizers, chemical pesticides, and concentrated feed used by conventional farmers and, as these products are fuel-intensive to produce, still employ these methods of being less dependent on fossil fuels. However, the increasing scale of a portion of organic operations will continue to move these operations further away from the organic agriculture tenet of a decreased dependence on fossil fuels and closer to a large-scale organics that resembles conventional farming in the way it is organized and operates. After all, the intensive use of irrigation systems, heavy machinery, and heated greenhouses are in themselves big energy users, whether they are taking place on an organic farm or a conventional one.

In order to help the organic farming community contend with the many issues and decisions now facing the rapidly growing and nationalized industry, the National Organic Standards Board (NOSB) discusses and makes recommendations on allowable substances for organic production, handling, and processing. The NOSB consists of 15 seats representing consumers, food processors, environmentalists, and organic farmers, all of whom have an interest in organic farming. However, even this independent board has to be protected against the influence of corporate pressure.

The transition of so much agriculture and industry to organics has been accompanied by the allowance of certain materials for use, specifying a sunset date, or a time by which it needs to be replaced. However, as illustrated by the controversial continued use of carrageenan, the influence of those who benefit from its use can make it difficult for the NOSB to enforce that sunset date, if not impossible.[13]

The composition of the board, too, needs to be safeguarded. Here again the Cornucopia Institute earns its watchdog status, having sued the USDA in early 2016 for filling the NOSBs organic farmer seats with non-farmers.[14]

And yet, these changes in organics do not signify complete control by big business of their newfound industry. All of these inroads into the organic food system, as well as the weakening of its commonly held though not nationally standardized beliefs, have led to the growth of alternative food labels and farming systems that seek to regain components that have been lost, or to set the bar higher or "beyond" organics. Whether the emphasis is on the environment, the conditions in which animals are raised and fed, or the proximity of food production to the consumer, it seems likely that there will be more of such labeling in the future. Such certifications include "Certified Naturally Grown," "Food Justice Certified," "Predator Friendly," "American Grassfed," and "Buy Fresh Buy Local."

Also, a handful of pioneer organic firms have thus far managed to resist attempted buy-outs on the processing level. Of particular pride is the fact that one of these firms is Eden Foods of Clinton, Michigan, which not only remains independent but also refuses to use the USDA organic seal

---

[13] The Cornucopia Institute. 2016. "Will Carrageenan Remain in Organic Food?" https://www.cornucopia.org/2016/06/will-carrageenan-remain-organic-food/.

[14] The Cornucopia Institute. 2016. "USDA Sued for Corporate Hijack of Organic Industry Governing Board." https://www.cornucopia.org/2016/04/usda-sued-corporate-hijack-organic-industry-governing-board/.

on their certified products as it represents a weakened standard of organics.[15]

When considering agricultural inputs, remember that (thus far) intellectual property protections do not apply to open-pollinated (or heirloom) seeds or heritage breeds of livestock, both of which are experiencing rapid growth and support. A significant bright light in this area is the current Open Source Seed Initiative (OSSI), a combined effort of farmer-breeders, academics, and other concerned persons to keep as many seed varieties as possible in the public domain. When a seed variety is OSSI-pledged, it means that all involved breeders, seed companies, and purchasers of said variety agree to The Four Seed Freedoms in any transfer of these seeds in the future. These freedoms are:

- The freedom to save or grow seed for replanting or for any other purpose.
- The freedom to share, trade, or sell seed to others.
- The freedom to trial and study seed and to share or publish information about it.
- The freedom to select or adapt the seed, make crosses with it or use it to breed new lines and varieties.

How has the organic landscape changed since the implementation of National Organic Standards? In short, at every level of the food system. An overwhelming collection of small retail and distribution co-ops have given way to a few large operations. There have been changes in the processing of many organic brands acquired by big business. At the very least, the purchase of many organic brands is no longer going to support the smaller-scale, environmentally concerned farmers it once did. There have

---

[15] Eden Foods. 2006. "Why Eden Foods Chooses Not to Use the USDA Seal." http://www.edenfoods.com/articles/view.php?articles_id=78.

also been changes at the agricultural inputs and food production level, and to how the agriculture is actually being carried out.

Still, these changes have all happened in the arena of what might now be termed "industrial organics." In answer to the question, "Who owns organics?", hopefully, truly, this can be regarded as referring to the organics that existed before there was any monetary benefit in being organic and will remain after the bubble of industrial organics has burst. The owners of organics will still be the self-reliant, seed saving farmers and gardeners (with or without certification) and the conscientious, informed, and loyal customers who have always owned organics. As long as they don't forget their responsibility.

Jessie Smith *is a Michigan State University alumna (B.S., Crop and Soil Sciences; M.S., Entomology) and freelance agricultural writer. She works at Nodding Thistle, her family's farm in Barry County, that has a history of organic gardening and farm marketing since 1984. The integrated farm includes small grain crops and hay, a small beef/dairy herd and chicken flock, and six acres containing vegetables, small fruits, herbs, and an orchard.*

Leah Smith *is a Michigan State University alumna (B.S., Crop and Soil Sciences) and freelance agricultural writer. She works at her family's farm, Nodding Thistle, which was certified organic for 25 years by the Organic Growers of Michigan (1984-2006), the Ohio Ecological Food and Farm Association (2007-2008), and Certified Naturally Grown (2009). The farm continues to grow vegetables and other products in the same familiar way, but is no longer certified.*

The Future of Organic Farming
In a Time of Global Warming

Maynard Kaufman

We do not know just when farming in Michigan will be seriously impacted by climate change, but we do know that other places are already suffering droughts or flooding attributed to global warming. We also know that greenhouse gases, mainly carbon dioxide, methane, and nitrous oxide, are accumulating in our atmosphere and as they help to trap the warmth of the sun, global temperatures are slowly rising.

These greenhouse gases are emitted when fossil fuels, such as coal, oil and gas, are burned, but emissions began much earlier from deforestation and soil erosion. The warming this causes is very slow, and the danger lies in the fact that global temperatures are rising so slowly that the prospect of global warming has lost its urgency. In 2007, 71% of Americans believed that burning fossil fuels caused global warming, but two years later this percentage was down to 51%.

People in this country are not inclined to change their energy-intensive lifestyle and so carbon dioxide, the main greenhouse gas, has increased from 280 parts per million before the Industrial era to about 400 ppm today. Eventually, of course, emissions of carbon dioxide must be reduced by using less fossil fuel energy and more renewable sources of energy, but that is not a likely possibility to solve the problem of climate change for the time being. A cultural malaise is gradually developing and is reflected in either the blatant denial of climate change or in the passive acceptance of climate change with its acquiescence of End Times, whether religious or secular.

The other possibility, besides reducing the use of fossil fuels, is getting carbon dioxide out of the atmosphere through the natural process of photosynthesis, and it is rejected by many scientific writers in our urban society even as it is affirmed by many others who know more about farming. It is this possibility that is explored in this essay. We do know that before the industrial era, organic matter, which is 58% carbon, had accumulated quite naturally in soils and plants and did not concentrate in the atmosphere. Prairie soils in our Great Plains had 10 to 20% of organic matter before they were plowed. Since farming began soils have lost 30 to 80% of their organic matter. Although carbon has always circulated through the atmosphere, the soil, and the oceans, the current excess in the atmosphere and in the oceans (which are being acidified as a result) and the loss of carbon from the soil, is caused both by destructive farming practices and the burning of fossil fuels.

These destructive practices include deforestation and the loss of organic matter as plowing for annual grain crops caused the oxidation of carbon in the soil and its escape as carbon dioxide. The loss of organic matter was much greater when chemicals for fertilizers and pest control were adopted. As Jack Kittredge, policy director of Northeast Organic Farming Association – Massachusetts, wrote in a 2015 White Paper on carbon restoration, "use of synthetic agricultural chemicals is destructive of soil carbon." The use of fossil fuels for the manufacture of agricultural inputs and for mechanization adds to the carbon emissions from agriculture. Rattan Lal, a soil scientist from Ohio State University who has written much on this topic, has suggested that "more carbon may have been emitted into the atmosphere from deforestation and land use conversion than from fossil fuel combustion until the end of the twentieth century." (Lal, Preface to *Geotherapy*, edited by Thomas Goreau, p. xvi.)

Can this carbon dioxide be returned to the soil as organic matter by better farming practices? This is what organic farmers have always tried to do, and they have recently been joined by soil scientists such as Lal, mentioned above, and many others. Some of them make extravagant claims, as when Allan Yeomans, in his book *Priority One,* says (p. 101) we could beat global warming "in well under ten years." This may be possible, but it assumes that the world's farmers will all become organic farmers immediately. And even Yeomans complains about the lobbying power of the fossil fuel industries as they resist a transition to organic farming.

In a special paper published a couple of years ago, the Rodale Institute provided a more carefully-reasoned statement of carbon sequestration through regenerative organic agricultural practices. It lends some support to Yeoman's claims, and, recognizing that not all farms will shift to organic methods, it states that "if we extrapolate to half rather than all of global pasture and cropland, transition to regenerative modes of production may sequester 55% (29GtCO2) of 2012 annual emissions." This is a bit over half of the total global emissions of greenhouse gases in 2012, so it is possible to sequester annual emissions of greenhouse gases in soils and plants.

Getting the excess greenhouse gases out of the atmosphere is more urgent than reducing the rate of burning fossil fuels because it helps to postpone the warming of the planet immediately even as it builds up soil fertility, which is the aim of organic farmers. And it is necessary for all of us as eaters if we remember that chemical fertilizers, which came into use to maintain yields after chemical farming methods had destroyed soil fertility, may not be as easily available and widely used in the future.

Organic methods are the alternative. Also, it is urgent to reduce greenhouse gases in the atmosphere because the warming they cause in turn causes the melting of methane hydrates in tundra and in the oceans, and these emissions of methane can add more warming very rapidly.

What the Rodale Institute calls "regenerative organic farming" includes some specific emphases that add up to a reformed method of organic farming. They are not proposing a simple return to the good old days of organic farming even though they still emphasize feeding the organisms in the soil rather than the plants. It is farming and gardening without any or very reduced tillage, along with temporary cover crops planted between the main crops to cover the soil and help to control weeds and erosion. It also depends on crop rotation, retention of crop residue on the soil, and the use of compost for fertilizer which helps to fix carbon in the soil as humus. All this adds up to a more management-intensive system which has to be adapted to different soil types and climate conditions.

Some critics have rejected the possibility of carbon sequestration in soil because they argue that the carbon would escape sooner rather than later. But, according to the Rodale paper, arbuscular mycorrhizal fungi secrete a protein called glomalin which remains in the soil for decades as a stable form of organic carbon. Mycorrhizal fungi can also be added in the soil to seedlings through inoculations especially in places where heavy tillage has destroyed the native population of fungi.

The Rodale paper mentions both cropland and global pasture, or grasslands, which include 40% of global land surface area. Efforts have been made recently, informed especially by the work of Allen Savory's Holistic Management System, to develop grazing methods that can restore these grasslands. These depend on the intensive grazing of ruminants in relatively small paddocks where large herds are pressured as by the presence of predators. Their hoofs help to mix their manure and dead grasses into the soil to replenish its organic matter. This process is described by Adam D. Sacks and colleagues in a long article entitled "Reestablishing the Evolutionary Grassland-Grazer Relationship to Restore Atmospheric Carbon Dioxide to Pre-industrial Levels" which is included in *Geotherapy*, edited by Thomas Goreau *et al.*

Another way to sequester carbon includes greater reliance on perennial crops as emphasized in Permaculture. This has been advocated by Eric Toensmeier in his recent book, *The Carbon Farming Solution: A Global Toolkit of Perennial Crops and Regenerative Agricultural Practices for Climate Change Mitigation and Food Security.* Because of their extensive roots and reduced need for tillage, perennial plants and trees can sequester more carbon in the soil than annual crops. This is also true of the perennial grains under development at the Land Institute co-founded by Wes Jackson. Tree crops can also be competitive with annuals in net productivity, as argued by J. Russell Smith in his book of 1950, *Tree Crops.* The shift to more perennials will happen, but it is a long-term process. In the meantime annual crops can be produced with regenerative organic methods.

The most comprehensive book on strategies for restoring carbon from the atmosphere to the soil is *Geotherapy,* published in 2015 and edited by Thomas J. Goreau, Ronal Larson and Joanna Campe. The first 100 pages of this 600 page book consists of introductory essays by the editors, and the following pages include about ten chapters on biochar and another ten chapters on techniques for the remineralization of soils and organic additives. Biochar is essentially charcoal which has been "energized" with organic matter and helps plants grow. The charcoal embodies carbon in a form that stays in the soil. Any organic matter can be burned in the absence of oxygen to form biochar. Certainly it should be a vital component in the effort to sequester carbon.

If it is indeed possible to restore carbon to the soil through organic farming methods, why is it not happening? (It does happen on organic farms, but they are few and easily ignored.) There are several obvious reasons why carbon sequestration in soil has not become public policy. First of all, although Goreau was present in 1989 as a Senior Scientific Affairs Officer when the United Nations Framework Convention on Climate Change was organized, he was unable to convince the UNFCCC to include soil as a sink for carbon even though it has four times more carbon than the atmosphere. This helps to explain why soil as a sink for excess carbon is not on the formal agenda for climate change. He argues, and *Geotherapy* provides the evidence, that "if managed responsibly pastures alone, agriculture alone, or reforestation alone could absorb much of the carbon dioxide increase" (p. 37).

But the reasons for the rejection of these natural solutions are deeper in our technological culture. We like to see immediate results and several so-called "geo-engineering" solutions have been proposed. But they are very expensive and none have been implemented. They include machines to scrub carbon dioxide from the atmosphere and bury it, mirrors in space to reflect sunlight, and albedo enhancement by injecting sulfate aerosols into the stratosphere. Needless to say, there is no guarantee that such expensive schemes will work, and the possibility exists that they could have horrendous unintended side effects. Such schemes are reviewed, critically, in books like *Fixing the Climate* by James Roger Fleming and *Earthmasters* by Clive Hamilton. They are mentioned here only to remind us that the prevalent technological mentality in America is impatient with natural methods that rely on photosynthesis.

Given the potential problems with geo-engineering technologies, a more recent book, in 2015, *Atmosphere of Hope* by Tim Flannery, proposes "third-way" technologies to solve the climate problem. "Third-way technologies re-create, enhance, or restore the processes that created the balance of greenhouse gases which existed prior to human interference, with the aim of drawing carbon, at scale, out of earth's atmosphere and/or oceans" (p. 151). These "technologies" certainly include what we call organic farming and reforestation in this paper. Flannery says these are "new," but only the term "third way" is new.

The emphasis on technology rather than on natural processes does imply a distrust of nature, and it also applies to organic farming, where it is reinforced by vested economic interests that make money on agricultural inputs such as pesticides and chemical fertilizers. The lure of money and the convenience it can buy seems to deter many of us from thinking about a sustainable way of life. We do need a shift in values. One such fundamental and necessary shift is to convince government leaders to move beyond their obsession with economic growth in the money economy as they continue to promote the production and burning of fossil fuels. How can we learn to recognize the illusory nature of money in comparison to the gifts of nature? How can we give up dreams of material progress and, instead, seek contentment in learning how to work with nature rather than to transform nature with technology? And how can we gear into the coming post-petroleum era, which opens opportunities for more people to be involved in food production and participation in the planting and harvesting of perennial plants and trees?

The good news is that these questions are in the minds of many people who, at least as consumers, are seeking local and organic food. The recent emergence of several thousand farmers markets and Community Supported Agriculture arrangements are making local and organic produce available. Many people would like to raise their own food as well, but lack the resources to do so. A guaranteed annual wage would help this happen in a time of massive unemployment. As we shift away from a culture dependent on fossil fuels, more energy will be supplied by human labor and perhaps draft animals, at least on the farm. Many of us who are gardeners are already familiar with this and find it is enjoyable work. The vision of an emerging agrarian culture is glimmering on the horizon, and it provides hope to an increasing number of people at a time when the future looks dark because urban civilization is in danger of collapse as the use of fossil fuel energy is constrained in a changing climate.

There will definitely be organic farming in our future. It is one of the essential strategies that can insure that we have a future, both because it can restore carbon from the atmosphere, where it is a pollutant, back into the soil, where it is a necessary nutrient that helps plants grow. Thus global warming is slowed and eventually stopped. Best of all, it thereby enriches the soil so that food can be grown without the chemicals that add to greenhouse gases in the atmosphere.

But to make this happen, those of us who identify with the organic movement must, first, be much more assertive about the need for organic farming, both as citizens individually, and as organic organizations. Although early organic thinkers challenged the industrial mode of farming, many of us now are content to do our own thing and have more recently become relatively non-political.

Second, the change must happen on a political level. Recognizing that this must be a large-scale shift, we must press for needed changes in agricultural policy at the highest level of government. This will be difficult because politicians want to favor the industries that support them. We will succeed only with long-term commitment.

Third, we must insist on the need for a paradigm shift to a post-petroleum reality, which means a gradual movement from an industrial to an agrarian culture, at least as far as food production is concerned. In this case the message is "change or die" before the planet becomes uninhabitable.

Fourth, this will be a change to a more humane society in which life can once again be enjoyable. We can move beyond a life in which frantic pursuit of money is necessary in order to buy stuff, to a life of contentment with what nature offers. Only in this way can we feel confident that a prosperous future is insured.

Bibliography

Bates, Albert, *The Biochar Solution: Carbon farming and Climate Change.* New Society Publishers, 2010.

Flannery, Tim, *Atmosphere of Hope.* Atlantic Monthly Press, 2016.

Fleming, James Roger, *Fixing the Sky: The checkered history of weather and climate control.* New York: Columbia University Press, 2010.

Goreau, Thomas, et. al., editors, *Geotherapy.* Boca Raton: CRC Press, 2015

Hamilton, Clive, *Earthmasters.* New Haven: Yale University Press, 2013

Kittredge, Jack, "Soil Carbon Restoration: Can Biology do the Job?" White Paper available at http://www.nofamass .org/sites/default/files/2015_White_Paper_web.pdf

Lal, R., J.M. Kimble, R.R. Follett, and C.V. Cole, *The Potential of U.S. Cropland to Sequester Carbon and Mitigate the Greenhouse Effect.* Boca Raton: Lewis Publishers, 1999.

Lehmann, Johannes, and Stephen Joseph, (editors) *Biochar for Environmental Management.* Earthscan, 2009.

Ohlson, Kristin, *The Soil Will Save Us*. Rodale Press, 2014.

Rodale Institute, "Regenerative Organic Agriculture and Climate Change," 2014.

Ruddiman, William F., *Plows, Plagues and Petroleum*. Princeton: Princeton University Press, 1999.

Schwartz, Judith D., *Cows Save the Planet*. Chelsea Green Publishing, 2013.

Sheperd, Mark, *Restoration Agriculture: Real world permaculture for farmers*. Austin, TX: Acres, USA, 2013.

Smith, J. Russell, *Tree Crops: A Permanent Agriculture*. New York: Devin Adair, 1950.

Toensmeier, Eric, *The Carbon Farming Solution*. White River Junction: Chelsea Green Publishing, 2016

White, Courtney, *Grass, Soil, Hope: A Journey Through Carbon Country*. Chelsea Green Publishers, 2014.

Yeomans, Allen, *Priority One: Together we can beat global warming*. Australia: Keyline Publishing Company, 2005.

About the Editors

Maynard Kaufman was born in 1929 and raised by Mennonite parents on a farm in South Dakota. After receiving his doctorate from the University of Chicago, he taught courses in Religion and Environmental Studies at Western Michigan University from 1963 to 1987.

In 1973 he was granted a half-time leave of  absence from classroom teaching to conduct a School of Homesteading on a farm suitable for this purpose near Bangor, Michigan. When Organic Growers of Michigan was organized that same year he had his farm "Certified Organic" and was soon active in the organic movement. In 1991-1992 he co-organized Michigan Organic Food and Farm Alliance.

He has published many articles on food, farming, and energy issues, and in 2008 he published *Adapting to the End of Oil: Toward an Earth-Centered Spirituality*.

In 2001 Maynard and his wife Barbara moved into the off-grid house powered by sun and wind they built on a part of their land so they could sell other parts of the farm and farm buildings to three younger organic growers. Thus they could retire from farming, but he still enjoys gardening to raise their food.

Julia Christianson grew up in Oklahoma City, Oklahoma, and received her B.A. from the University of Virginia in 1974. A lifetime organic gardener, she spent her career in non-profit administration in the Washington, D.C. area, retiring as Administrative Director of ICON Community Services, an organization which provided people with severe disabilities the support they needed to live and work as integrated, contributing members of the community.

She and her husband moved to Michigan in 2010, settling on a few acres east of Decatur. She joined MOFFA in 2010 and has served as the organization's "very part-time" administrative staff since January, 2013.

Photo Credits

Page 9   OGM Field Day led by Bruce Shultz at the School of Homesteading.[1]

Page 11   Earth Day at Bronson Park in Kalamazoo.

Page 13   OGM logo.

Page 14   OGM "Certified Organic" label.

Page 18   OGM Field Day at the School of Homesteading, 1978

Page 20   OGM Metal Farm Sign.

Page 42   George Bird and Pat Whetham at Harvest Festival in Grand Rapids, 2003. Photo from the MOFFA archives.

Page 44   The mobile processing trailer at the Ware Farm, 2003. Photo from the MOFFA archives.

Page 48   MOFFA Logo created in 1994 by Laura B. DeLind.

Page 50   First Edition of *Eating Organically*, 1995.

Page 65   John Hooper at the MOFFA booth, 2014. Photo by Vicki Morrone.

Page 68   John Biernbaum before the National Organic Standards Board, 2016. *Courtesy Cornucopia Institute.*

Page 95   Organic Farmers of Michigan Field Day, 2015. Photo by Julia Christianson

Page 108   OGM – MLT Field Day, 1981.

Page 129   Oryana Food Co-op Members. *Courtesy Oryana Food Co-op.*

Page 131   Photo of Mike Williams, Oryana General Manager, 1980. *Courtesy Oryana Food Co-op.*

Page 183   Photo of Maynard Kaufman by Jon Towne.

Page 184   Photo of Julia Christianson by John Biernbaum.

---

[1] Photos by Maynard Kaufman unless otherwise identified.

Appendix A:
Timeline of the Organic Movement
Maynard Kaufman and Julia Christianson

(As editors we felt the need for some sort of overview of the organic movement, especially that part of the movement that preceded Organic Growers of Michigan. We hope the following timeline can serve this purpose.)

To begin with, the organic movement was informed by European and American researchers and scientific writers who began publishing books that were critical of the rapid adoption of chemical fertilizers and pesticides that became available over the past one hundred years. Some of these books and events are listed below.

1890s: George Washington Carver was one of the first Americans to promote what have become known as organic methods.   He used the term regenerative agriculture, emphasizing the use of compost rather than artificial fertilizers, crop rotation, and cover crops. He taught at the Tuskegee Institute for 47 years, beginning in 1896.

1909: Fritz Haber and Carl Bosch successfully demonstrated the artificial process for creating ammonia, the key ingredient for making various forms of synthetic nitrogen.

1922: The Capper-Volstead Act permitted agricultural producers to form an association for cooperative marketing and to set prices, subject to certain restrictions, in an exception to the Sherman Anti-Trust Act of 1890.

1924: Rudolf Steiner, the founder of Biodynamics, presented a series of eight lectures, which he titled "Agriculture Course." Although Steiner died only a year later, his teachings were carried on by Ehrenfried Pfeiffer, who promoted them widely in Europe and in the United States. Because Steiner's ideas were perceived as somewhat mystical in this country, they found only limited acceptance, but "Biodynamics" continues as one version of organic farming.

1938: Dr. William Albrecht, a soil scientist and agronomist, published *Loss of Soil Organic Matter and its Restoration*. His research has been widely promoted in the periodical *Acres USA*.

1940: Walter James, Fourth Baron Northbourne, published *Look to the Land,* in which he was the first to apply the term "organic" to this method of farming.

1940: Sir Albert Howard, one of the founders of organic agriculture, published *An Agricultural Testament,* which explored soil fertility and the importance of composting at a time when synthetic inputs were growing in use.

1942: J.I. Rodale began to publish *Organic Gardening and Farming Magazine*, largely inspired by Sir Albert Howard's research. Rodale's magazine did much to popularize organic farming.

1943: Lady Eve Balfour published *The Living Soil*, which describes the results of the first three years of the Haughley Experiment, the first long-term, side-by-side scientific comparison of organic and chemical-based farming.

1945: Following the end of World War II, the use of synthetic fertilizers and pesticides expanded rapidly. The capacity of synthetic nitrogen fertilizer to function as an explosive was already known during World War I, but it was widely used in World War II when it was manufactured in massive quantities. After the war the surplus nitrate fertilizer contributed enormously to the spread of the so-called "Green Revolution", along with biocides, many of which were also developed as part of the war effort, now functioning to kill pests.

1953: Five of the many Rodale-inspired organic garden clubs that had been active for several years in Michigan banded together to form the Federated Organic Clubs of Michigan.

1962: Publication of Rachel Carson's book *Silent Spring,* in which she demonstrated the negative impacts of pesticides such as DDT on bird populations. The book was very popular and helped to galvanize the environmental movement of the 1960s and 70s. It also encouraged organic farmers to refuse chemical pesticides.

1963: Ruth Stout publicized the importance of mulching, especially in her book, *Gardening Without Work,* so that tillage can be avoided and soil moisture can be conserved.

1972: IFOAM (International Federation of Organic Agricultural Movements) formed in Versailles, France, to help in the coordination of standards for organic certification.

1973: Organic Growers of Michigan formed in Southwest Michigan. Eventually at least 13 chapters were active in different parts of Michigan at different times.

1980: The USDA under President Carter released a preliminary "Report and Recommendations on Organic Farming" (the Bergland Report), which was promptly suppressed in 1981 by the incoming Reagan administration.

1990: In October, the Organic Foods Production Act became law as part of the farm bill. The OFPA was championed by Senator Patrick Leahy of Vermont, and was drafted largely through the efforts of Leahy staffer Kathleen Merrigan.

1991: Efforts by organic leaders in Michigan to start an organic organization that could receive tax-deductible contributions resulted in the beginnings of what came to be known as Michigan Organic Food and Farm Alliance, (MOFFA), incorporated in January, 1992.

1992: MOFFA board member Merrill Clark was among those who were appointed to the first National Organic Standards Board (NOSB). They held their first meeting in October.

1997: In December, following five years of contentious discussion among the members of the National Organic Standards Board, the first proposed rule for organic production was published by the USDA. The rule met with widespread condemnation from organic farmers, particularly in three areas—it permitted the use of sewage sludge (biosolids); it approved the use of genetically modified organisms (in opposition to the recommendations of the NOSB); and it permitted irradiation of foods—and the USDA went back to the drawing board.

2000: A final proposed rule was published in December. The rule has been revised and expanded in the years since, but it is essentially the rule that governs the use of the "organic label" today.

2002: Federally accredited certifying agents began certifying organic operations in April; by October the rule was fully implemented.

2006: Following the implementation of the Federal organic rule in 2002, OGM agreed to seek federal accreditation as a certifying agency, but after careful deliberation it was considered to be too difficult by leaders of the certification program, and OGM was dissolved in 2006.

Appendix B
MOFFA Board Members 1992-2017

Maynard Kaufman, 1992-2006, chair 1992-1997, secretary 1997-2002

Merrill Clark, 1992-2002, chair 1997-1999, co-chair 2000, vice-chair 2002, secretary 1992-1997

John Valenti, 1992-1994, treasurer 1992-1993

Pat Whetham, 1992-2010, vice-chair 1991-1999, chair 1999-2000, treasurer 2004

Grey Larison, 1992-1997; 2000-2003, treasurer 1993-1997; 2001-2003

Laura DeLind, 1992-1999

Betty Edmunds, 1993-2001, treasurer 1997-2001, administrative director 1997-2001

Barney & Delores Wall, 1993-1994

Paul Scott, 1994-1996

Jane Bush, 1995-1997

April Allison, 1996-1999

Susan Houghton, 1996-2000, vice-chair 1999-2000

Gita Posselt, 1996-1999

Sharon Renier, 1996-1998

Kathy Houston, 1997-2000

Richard Harwood, 1998

Carl McIlvain, 1999-2000

Carol Osborne, 1999-2005, co-chair 2000, chair 2001-2003, administrative director 2004-2006

Gail Campana, 2000-2001

David Dingeman, 2000-2000

Jan Ryan, 2000-2002

Nancy Jones Keiser, 2001-2009

Lisa Wesala, 2001-2004

Jim Bingen, 2002-2010, chair 2005-2010

George Bird, 2002-2010, treasurer 2008-2010, secretary 2009, co-chair 2010

Carolyn Koch, 2002-2005, secretary 2002-2005
Doug Murray, 2002-2009, vice-chair 2003, co-chair 2005-2006
Rick Samyn, 2002
Suzanne Smucker, 2002-2005, chair 2004-2005
Cindy Garber, 2004, treasurer 2004
Claire O'Leary Maitre, 2004-2005, secretary 2004-2005
Kurt Cobb, 2005-2008, treasurer 2005-2007
Barb Mutch, 2005-2007, secretary 2005
John VanVoorhees, 2005
Emily Reardon, 2006-2008, secretary 2006-2008
Taylor Reid, 2006-2009, co-chair 2006-2007, vice-chair 2008
Suzanne Rutkowski, 2007-2008
Chris Bardenhagen, 2008-2015, treasurer 2013-2015
Yvette Berman, 2008-2014, co-chair 2010, treasurer 2010-
    2012
Matt Grieshop, 2008-2011
Diana Jancek, 2008-2009
John Biernbaum, 2009-present, chair 2016-present[1]
John Hooper, 2009-present, chair 2011-2015, secretary
    2017-present
Vicki Morrone, 2009-present, secretary 2011-2014
Les Roggenbuck, 2009-2012
Timothy Fischer, 2010, co-chair 2010
Paul Keiser, 2010
Lee Arboreal, 2012-2015
Melissa Hornaday, 2012
Carolyn Lowry, 2012-2014
Linda Jackson Torony, 2012-2015
Julia Studier, 2013-present, secretary 2016
Dane Terrill, 2013-present, treasurer 2016-present
Dan Bewersdorff, 2014-present
Karen Warner, 2014-2015, secretary 2014-2015
Dan Rossman, 2015-present, vice-chair 2016-present
Emily Shettler, 2016-present
Amy Newday, 2016-present
Emily Nicholls, 2016-present

---

[1] "Present" as of publication of this book in May 2017.

Appendix C:
Grants Received by MOFFA 1992-2017

Most of the grants listed below were meant to fund ongoing operations. Grants made to fund specific projects are indicated in the footnotes.

1993	Center for Science in the Public Interest	$ 2,250
1994	National Coalition Against Misuse of Pesticides	500
1994	Michigan Land Trustees[1]	10,000
1994	Whole Foods (5% of day's receipts)	1,152
1995	USDA-SARE[2]	1,000
1995	Michigan Department of Agriculture	1,500
1995	Michigan Department of Agriculture	1,500
1996	Michigan Agricultural Stewardship Assn.	500
1997	American Health and Nutrition	500
1997	Eden Foods	1,000
1997	Michigan Land Trustees	3,900
1998	Michigan Agricultural Extension Service[3]	70,000
1998	Michigan Department of Agriculture	5,000
1998	Michigan Land Trustees	3,100
1998	USDA-SARE[4]	23,969
1999	USDA-SARE[5]	41,000
1999	Harris Foundation	500
2001	Harris Foundation	500
2001	Michigan Department of Agriculture[6]	20,000

---

[1] Seed money to fund an executive director position.

[2] In support of the first Michigan Organic Harvest Festival at Washtenaw Community College near Ypsilanti.

[3] Funding secured by John Fisk for a three-year on-farm research project.

[4] Funding for a survey of Community Supported Agriculture in Michigan, Indiana, and Ohio, conducted by Laura B. DeLind.

[5] Funds to purchase and outfit a mobile food processing trailer, secured by Susan Houghton.

2002	Michigan Land Trustees	1,500
2002	Michigan Land Trustees	1,000
2002	Michigan Department of Agriculture[7]	20,000
2003	Michigan Land Trustees	1,000
2004	Michigan Land Trustees	1,500
2004	Fetzer Fund	1,500
2004	ECCO/MEC	3,750
2008	Rhonda Fackert[8]	10,000
2013	The Offield Family Foundation	10,000
2013	MI Dept. of Agriculture and Rural Development[9]	39,158
2015	SARE 'Mini-Grant'	1,500
2016	SARE 'Mini-Grant'	1,500
2017	SARE 'Mini-Grant'[10]	1,500

[6] Michigan Organic Conference in 2001, secured by Carol Osborne.

[7] Michigan Organic Conference 2002, secured by Carol Osborne.

[8] This donation provided funds for the 2008 Michigan Organic Conference as well as the "Collaborative Alliance for Michigan Food and Farming" project.

[9] "High Tunnel Grant" conducted by Gregory Lang and Eric Hanson at MSU, 2013-2015.

[10] The SARE 'Mini-Grants' in 2015-2017 subsidized attendance at the Organic Intensives educational event for Michigan educators and Extension personnel.

Appendix D:
Awards Presented by MOFFA

Lifetime Achievement
    2000   Maynard Kaufman
    2001   Richard Harwood
    2002   Joe Scrimger
    2003   Merrill Clark
    2004   Betty Edmunds
    2005   Grey Larison
    2006   George Bird
    2010   Doug Murray and Nancy Jones-Keiser

Public Service
    2000   Christine Lietzau
    2001   Susan Smalley
    2002   Senator Leon Stille
    2003   Dan Rossman
    2004   John Biernbaum
    2005   Dale Mutch
    2006   Joe Scrimger, Bio-Systems/Life Time Foods

Community Service
    2000   People's Food Co-op Ann Arbor
    2001   East Lansing Food Co-op
    2002   Healthy Traditions Network
    2003   Oryana Community Co-op
    2004   Michelle Lutz
    2005   People's Food Co-op Kalamazoo/Chris Dilley
    2006   Carol Osborne
    2007   Rhonda Fackert
    2008   Bernie and Sandee Ware, Ware Farms

Volunteer of the Year
   2000   April Allison
   2001   Pat Whetham
   2002   John Masterson and Patty Withey
   2003   Laura DeLind
   2004   Jim Bingen
   2005   Brian Thomas
   2006   Emily Reardon
   2007   Kurt Cobb

Farmer of the Year
   2006   Michelle and Danny Lutz, Maple Creek Farm
   2007   John and Patti Warnke
   2008   Jim and Pat Graham and Family, Graham Farms
   2010   Jim Koan, Almar Orchards
   2011   Lee and Laurie Arboreal, Eaters' Guild

Appendix E:
Glossary of Acronyms

501(c)(3).....IRS designation for a non-profit educational organization
AAM ....American Agriculture Movement
AES...........Agricultural Experiment Station
ANR..........Agriculture and Natural Resources [Week at MSU]
CANR ....College of Agriculture and Natural Resources [at MSU]
CEC ....Cation Exchange Capacity [soil test]
CES...........Cooperative Extension Service
CSA...........Community Supported Agriculture
FFM..........Fair Food Matters [in Kalamazoo]
GE.............Genetically Engineered, or Genetic Engineering
GFK ....Good Food Kalamazoo
GLEXPO ...Great Lakes Fruit and Vegetable Expo
GMG ....Growing Matters Garden [in Kalamazoo]
GMO ....Genetically Modified Organism
HTRC ....Horticulture Teaching and Research Center [at MSU]
IFOAM ......International Federation of Organic Agricultural
               Movements
IPM...........Integrated Pest Management
LETS ....Local Exchange Trading System
LISA ....Low Input Sustainable Agriculture [a program
               authorized in the 1985 Farm Bill]
LTHF.........Land Trust Homesteading Farm
MASA ....Michigan Agricultural Stewardship Association
MDA ....Michigan Department of Agriculture [1921-2011]
MDARD.....Michigan Department of Agriculture and Rural
               Development [2011-]
MIFFS ....Michigan Integrated Food and Farming Systems
MLT..........Michigan Land Trustees
MOAC........Michigan Organic Advisory Committee
MOC ....Michigan Organic Connections [newsletter]
MOC ....Michigan Organic Conference
MOFFA .....Michigan Organic Food and Farm Alliance
MOFGA .....Maine Organic Farmers and Gardeners Association
MOGAP .....Michigan Organic Grower Advancement Project
               [became MOFFA shortly after its inception]
MOSES......Midwest Organic and Sustainable Education Services
MSU ....Michigan State University

MSUE........Michigan State University Extension
NMSFC .....Northern Michigan Small Farm Conference
NOAP ....National Organic Action Plan
NOFA ....Northeast Organic Farming Association
NOP...........National Organic Program
NOSB ....National Organic Standards Board
NRCS........Natural Resources Conservation Service [a program
of the USDA]
OCIA..........Organic Crop Improvement Association
OFM ....Organic Farmers of Michigan
OFPA.........Organic Foods Production Act (1990)
OFRF.........Organic Farming Research Foundation
OFTP.........Organic Farmer Training Program [of the Student
Organic Farm at MSU]
OGM..........Organic Growers of Michigan
OSSI ....Open Source Seed Initiative
PVPA.........Plant Variety Protection Act
SARE.........Sustainable Agricultural Research and Education [a
program of the USDA]
SOF............Student Organic Farm
UNFCCC...United Nations Framework Convention on Climate
Change
UNFI ....United Natural Foods Incorporated
UPREC......Upper Peninsula Research and Education Center
USDA ....United States Department of Agriculture
WMU ....Western Michigan University

Index

A Sense of Wonder 49
Acres USA 157, 187
*Adapting to the End
  of Oil* 183
AgHub 140
Albrecht, William 5, 187
Allison, April..... 40, 190, 195
Almar Orchards...............195
American Agriculture
  Movement 143
American Grassfed..........169
American Health and
  Nutrition 192
An Agricultural Testament
 187
Anderson, Arden.............158
Ann Arbor, MI 17, 125,
  129, 132
Appetite for Change 127
Appelhof, Mary 7, 8
Arboreal, Lee 191
Arboreal, Lee and Laurie ..195
Argentine, MI 33
Atmosphere of Hope 178

Balfour, Lady Eve........5, 187
Bangor, MI 106, 107, 109,
  114, 115, 183
Bardenhagen, Chris 191
Barrett, Paul......................75
Bartell, Eric 129
Bath, MI 32
Battel, Bob 78
Bauer, Charles.............21, 22
Baughman, Brad 78
Bedford, Chris....................56
beginningfarmers.org......137
Behe, Bridget 75
Belasco, Warren...............127
Berden, Dean 28, 93
Bergland Report . 71, 79, 188

Bergland, Bob 188
Berman, Yvette......... 65, 191
Bewersdorff, Dan............ 191
Biernbaum, John 56, 75,
  76, 81, 87, 91, 92, 191, 194
Bingen, Jim 43, 51, 61, 64,
  75, 76, 84, 87, 104, 190,
  195
Biodynamics...... 79, 186, 187
Bio-Systems 72, 143, 158
Bird, George ... 42, 59, 64, 70,
  75, 79, 80, 84, 87, 190, 194
Blahnik, Lynne 38, 39, 40
Bober, Rita and Norm 114
Bohannen, Lisa................. 75
Bolleber, Luise 126, 136
Bosch, Carl 186
Bosma, Anna..................... 86
Bowden, Tom and Lynn ... 31
Boyne City, MI 3, 132
Brabanec, John and Julia ..134
Brewer, Mike 87
Brighton, MI 132
Brown, Elaine 87
Buchanan, James 32
Bush, Jane 31, 190
Buy Fresh Buy Local...... 169
Buying clubs 128

Campana, Gail.......... 41, 190
Campe, Joanna 176
Can-Do Kitchen 58, 115
Capper-Volstead Act 95, 186
Carbon Media Group...... 140
Carmody Farm.................. 22
Carmody, Steve................. 22
Carmody, Steve and
  Kathleen........................ 22
Caro, MI 29
Carson, Rachel... 49, 71, 128,
  188

Carver, George Washington 186
Cassopolis, MI......................3
Cavigelli, Michael..............75
Center for Food Safety 68
Center for Science in the Public Interest 192
Certification....... 7, 9, 10, 14, 15, 18, 20, 21, 28, 32, 34, 45, 121, 124, 135
Certified Naturally Grown 169
Chaprnka, John.................32
Christianson, Julia.......3, 66, 100, 117, 123, 184, 186
Cinzori Family Farm.........20
Clark, John 54
Clark, John and Merrill ...19, 72
Clark, Merrill....... 13, 38, 39, 41, 42, 51, 52, 53, 100, 190, 194
Clark, Sean 75
Clarksville, MI....................54
Climbing Mt. Organic: An Ecosystem Approach to Pest Management..........79
Clinton County, MI 31
Clio, MI 31
Cobb, Kurt.............. 191, 195
Coldwater, MI......................3
Coleman, Eliot 71, 89
Collier, Colleen 104
Community Connections.107
Community Supported Agriculture. 31, 45, 49, 76, 83, 85, 86, 89, 111, 117, 178
Community Vibrations....132
Concentration and Power in the Food System: Who Controls What We Eat? ..159
Cooper, William 71
Corbin, Andrew..................75

Cornucopia Institute ... 2, 57, 163, 164
Crockett, Jim 130
Crull, Heather................. 112
CSA.............. *See* Community Supported Agriculture

Dahlberg, Ken......... 105, 115
Davenport, John 75
Davis Dairy 27
Davis, Adelle 128
Davis, Nelson and Ann..... 27
Davison, MI....................... 31
Dawson, Ken 27
Decatur, MI........... 7, 16, 184
DeLind, Laura 39, 40, 41, 42, 45, 47, 50, 54, 55, 72, 74, 75, 84, 115, 117, 190, 192, 195
Detroit, MI 3, 29, 42, 78, 87, 125
DeVries, James........... 21, 22
Dillon, Matthew.............. 165
Dingeman, David........... 190
Donahue, Brian................ 84
Down to Earth................. 23
DuPont 165
Dyer, Larry 75

Earthmasters 177
East Lansing Food Co-op ...194
Eastown Food Co-op 21
Eater's Pledge 59
Eaters' Guild................... 195
Eating Organically ...42, 49, 62
Eaton County, MI 31
Eco-Farm, An Acres USA Primer.......................... 157
Eden Foods........ 27, 169, 192
Edens, Thomas 27, 71
Edible Flint 87
Edmunds, Betty 41, 66, 190, 194
Edson, Charles.................. 75

Electrolytes, the Spark of Life..................................158
Elmendorf, George..............23
Erich Wesjohann Group..166
ETC Group........................166

Fackert, Rhonda 194
Fair Food Matters 58, 114, 115
Family Farms Conference ...58
Fanning Soil Service 24
Farm Guide........62, 124, *See also Eating Organically*
Farm to Consumer Foundation....................158
Farmer's Pledge.... 59, 60, 62
Farmers markets.......29, 178
Farms of Tomorrow Revisited..........................84
Fedco Seeds........................57
Federated Organic Clubs...3, 188
Ferrarese, Michelle 83, 86
Ferris, Richard 31
Fetzer Fund 193
Field Crop Ecology 157
Fields of Learning: The Student Farm Movement in North America...........91
Filonowicz, Jan.................106
Filonowicz, Joseph C. 105, 107, 109
Fischer, Timothy 65, 191
Fisk, John 45, 75
Fixing the Climate 177
Flannery, Tim...................178
Fleming, James Roger.....177
Flint, MI 57, 87
Flushing MI 37
Fogiel, Andy.........................86
Food Justice Certified 169
Fordos, Ernie 93
Fowlerville, MI 41
Frog Holler..........................17
From the Soil Up 157

Gage, Stuart...................... 75
Garber, Cindy 191
Gardening Without Work...188
Geisler, Barbara 115, 183
Genesee County, MI 4, 31, 32, 37
Genetically Modified Organisms... 55, 67, 68, 91
Geotherapy 174, 176, 177
Giving Tree Farm 83
GLEXPO.... 44, 59, 77, 78, 80
Glick, Bob.......................... 32
Glick, Bob and Eleanor 30
Gluck, Ben......................... 86
Good Food Kalamazoo.... 114
Goreau, Thomas..... 174, 176, 177
Gould, Charles 78
Graham Farms 195
Graham, Jim and Pat..... 195
Grain Train Natural Foods Market.............. 132
Grand Rapids Farmers Market........................... 21
Grand Rapids, MI 3, 10, 42, 44, 114
Great Lakes Fruit and Vegetable Expo ....*See* GLEXPO
Green Revolution............ 187
Green Tree Cooperative Grocery 132
Greening of Detroit........... 87
Grey Cat Farm................. 22
Grieshop, Matt..... 75, 77, 79, 191
Grigg, Linda.................... 129
Groh, Trager 84
Grose, Steve 32
Grosse Pointe, MI 3
Growing Connections Festival.......................... 53
Growing in Place Community Farm .. 50, 82, 84

Growing Matters
    Garden................. 112, 115
Gussow, Joan 49
Gut, Larry 75

Haber, Fritz 186
Hall, Roger and Charlene 23
Hamilton, Clive 177
Hamm, Michael 76, 77
Hampshire Farm 29
Hampshire, Randy and
    Shirley 29
Hancock, MI.....................131
Hannah, John 70
Hanson, Eric 78, 193
Harris Foundation...........192
Harris, Craig.....................27
Harvest Festivals .. 5, 41, 42,
    53, 74, 111
Harwood, Richard.......27, 45,
    71, 72, 73, 75, 76, 82, 84,
    97, 190, 194
Haynes, Chuck...................31
Haynes, Dean.....................71
Haynes, George W. 4
Healthy People, Places,
    and Communities 112
Healthy Traditions
    Network........... 42, 53, 194
Hefferan, Tara 118
Hemenway, Dan 108
Henderson, Elizabeth 49, 56
Hendrix Genetics.............166
Hepperly, Paul...................79
Herpolsheimer, Chuck 29
Hillsdale County, MI........26
Hillsdale Natural Grocery
   132
Hillsdale, MI 3, 24, 132
Holmes, Robert 107
Holt High School..................5
Hooper, John............. 65, 191
Hornaday, Melissa 191
Horticulture Teaching and
    Research Center 82

Houghton, Susan 31, 42,
    44, 83, 190, 192
Houston, Kathy............... 190
Howard, Craig................... 31
Howard, Philip H............. 159
Howard, Sir Albert 187
Hubbardston, MI 3
Hudson, MI 23
Huraczy, Mike and Linda 24
Hydroponics 68

IFOAM........... 11, 19, 27, 188
Imlay City, MI 29
In Harmony Farms .. 21, 22, 23
Ingham County, MI ... 5, 31, 41
Ingham, Elaine 2
Institute for Responsible
    Technology 57
Integrated Pest
    Management 71, 72
Ionia Natural Foods Co-op
    132
Ionia, MI........................... 132
Iowa State University
    Leopold Center............. 79
IPM ....See Integrated Pest
    Management
Irish-Brown, Amy 75
Ironwood, MI................... 132
Isaacs, Rufus 78
Isleib, Jim......................... 78

Jackson, Dana................... 49
Jackson, Linda 191
Jackson, MI 132
Jackson, Wes................... 176
James, Walter 187
Jancek, Diana 191
Johnson, Trevor 86
Jones, Christine................. 2
Jones, Frank and Kay 31
Jost, Solomon 86

Kalamazoo Community
    Gardens Initiative 111

Kalamazoo, MI......3, 42, 112, 114, 132
Kastel, Mark.......................57
Kaufman, Maynard........1, 7, 8, 16, 38, 39, 42, 55, 64, 93, 105, 114, 115, 172, 183, 186, 190, 194
Kaufman, Maynard and Sally.........................24, 106
Kaufman, Sally.....19, 20, 39, 107
Keep Growing Detroit.......87
Keewanau Co-op..............131
Keiser, Nancy Jones...43, 57, 64, 84, 190, 194
Keiser, Paul 100, 191
Kellogg Foundation...........82
Kidwell, Bob and Linda ...23, 24, 26
King, Lewis and Bea 27
Kingston, MI.......................29
Kirschenmann, Fred 79
Kittredge, Jack 173
Kloppenburg, Jack Jr........49
Koan, Jim...........................195
Koch, Carolyn 191
Koenig, Herman 71
Kunkle, Dale.......................31

Lal, Rattan........................173
Land Institute...................176
Land Trust Homesteading Farm... 106, 107, 108, 109, 111
Lang, Gregory...................193
Lansing Community College............................88
Lansing Urban Farm Project 50
Lansing, MI.................3, 4, 31
Larison, Grey........12, 14, 21, 39, 42, 190, 194
Larison, Grey and Judy 22
Larson, Ronal 176
Lawn, C.R. 57

Lawrence, MI 59
Lawton, MI.......................114
Leahy, Patrick 188
Leatherman-Walker, Jayne 83
Lee Baker Farm..............110
Lee, Kaiulani 49
Lehnert, Dick.............18, 54
Leonard, Cliff and Bessie.....27
Leonard, Tim and Robyn 31
Lietzau, Christine.... 45, 104, 194
Lindquist, Jerry................78
Link, Terry........................54
Livingston County, MI 31
Livingston Organic Food Co-op............................132
Local Exchange Trading System 109
Local Harvest...................124
Logsdon, Gene...................24
Long, Jessica 86
Look to the Land 187
Lord Northbourne............*See* James, Walter
Loss of Soil Organic Matter and its Restoration 187
Lowry, Carolyn 191
Luttenbacher Greenhouse 31
Lutz, Michelle 194
Lutz, Michelle and Danny .195

MacKellar, Bruce..............75
Madsen, E.L. 4
Maine Organic Farmers and Gardeners Association . 26
Maitre, Claire .. *See* O'Leary, Claire
Malcomnson, Rob.............. 31
Maple Creek Farm 195
Marcellus, MI................... 23
Marks, Ed.......................... 38
Marlette, MI.................... 158
Marquette Food Co-op.... 131
Marquette, MI......... 125, 131
Martindale, Bobbi... 106, 109

Martlew, Gillian 158
Mason, MI 82, 84
Masterson, John 195
Mayville, MI 27
McArthur, Sandi 133, 136
McCraney, Ray 3
McFadden, Steven 84
McFarlan, Ashley 89
McIlvain, Carl 190
McKibben, Bill 115
MDA .... See Michigan
    Department of Agriculture
MDARD .... See Michigan
    Department of Agriculture
Meisner, Lynn 31
Merrigan, Kathleen .. 74, 188
Meyers, Sid 27
Michalik, Patricia 72
Michigan Agricultural
    Stewardship
    Association 192
Michigan Council of
    Humanities 108
Michigan Department of
    Agriculture 41, 43, 45,
    52, 54, 57, 62, 72, 100,
    192, 193
    Organic Registry 52
Michigan Department of
    Natural Resources 166
Michigan Environmental
    Council 59, 193
Michigan Farmers Union 53
Michigan Farmers Union
    Foundation 118
Michigan Federation of Food
    Co-ops 130
Michigan Field Crop
    Ecology 73, 74
Michigan Integrated Food
    and Farming Systems .. 43,
    58, 87, 88, 141
Michigan Land Trustees .. 40,
    105, 192, 193

Michigan Organic
    Conference 53, 55, 74,
    75, 90, 103
Michigan Organic
    Connections 40, 51, 58,
    62, 67, 68, 74
Michigan Organic Dairy
    Group 53
Michigan Organic Food and
    Farm Alliance 13, 20,
    37, 38, 51, 74, 84, 100,
    110, 111, 112, 115, 141,
    184, 189
Michigan Organic Grower
    Advancement Project... 13,
    39
Michigan Organic News ... 40
Michigan Organic Products
    Act 52, 53, 101, 103
Michigan Organic Survey ... 60,
    61
Michigan State University 4,
    19, 27, 43, 45, 53, 54, 57,
    61, 70, 97, 101, 108, 141,
    159
    Agricultural Experiment
        Station 54
    ANR Week .. 11, 19, 27, 41,
        45, 48, 54, 57, 67, 73,
        74, 103
    C.S. Mott Chair of
        Sustainable
        Agriculture 73, 76, 77
    Center for Regional Food
        Systems 77
    Center for Urban Food
        Systems 78
    Clarkesville Research
        Station 77
    College of Agriculture and
        Natural Resources 91
    Department of Community,
        Agriculture, Recreation,
        and Resource Studies, 137

Department of
Horticulture 76
Extension 24, 41, 42,
43, 45, 54, 57, 70, 75,
89, 112, 157, 192, 193
Horticulture Teaching and
Research Center ..83, 85
North Farm 89, 90, 91
Organic Day 54
Organic Farmer Training
Program 77, 83, 88
Student Organic Farm .58,
76, 78, 81
Sustainable Campus
Initiative 55
UPREC...........................89
Michigan Thumb Organics
......................................158
Middleton, Tom 75
MIFFS .... See Michigan
Integrated Food and
Farming Systems
Milarch, David.........128, 130
Mills, Stephanie.................49
Mobile Food Processing
Trailer 44, 58, 192
MOC ..See Michigan Organic
Conference, See Michigan
Organic Connections
MOFFA .... See Michigan
Organic Food and Farm
Alliance
MOGAP .... See Michigan
Organic Grower
Advancement Project
Moghtader, Jeremy 77
Monroe, Fred 86
Monroe, MI 3, 24
Monsanto 55, 68, 165
Montri, Adam 86, 87
Morey, Christopher 130
Morrone, Vicki 75, 77, 118,
191
MOSES..........................66, 76
Moyer, Jeff 56, 79

Moyer-Weber, Kathy 129
MSUE .... See Michigan State
University: Extension
Mt. Morris, MI 3
Mt. Pleasant, MI............. 132
Mundt, Bill....................... 23
Murray, Doug..... 57, 64, 191,
194
Murray, Seth..................... 86
Muskegon, MI 3
Mutch, Barb 191
Mutch, Dale......... 75, 87, 194

Nance, Steve 135
National Coalition Against
Misuse of Pesticides...... 192
National Farmers Union 118
National Organic Action
Plan Summit................. 63
National Organic
Program....... 51, 68, 73, 74
National Organic
Standards..................... 160
National Organic Standards
Board 15, 52, 68, 69,
133, 134, 189
Newday, Amy.................. 191
Newport, MI....................... 3
Ngouajio, Mathieu............ 87
Nicholls, Emily 191
NMSFC............ See Northern
Michigan Small Farm
Conference
Nodding Thistle Farm 78
NOFASee Northeast Organic
Farming Association
North Branch, MI 27, 29
North Farm ..... See Michigan
State University:North
Farm
Northeast Organic Farming
Association 59, 173
Northern Michigan Small
Farm Conference 58, 76

Northwind Natural Foods
    Co-op..............................132
NOSB . *See* National Organic
    Standards Board
Novi, MI 89

O'Leary, Claire 55, 191
Oakland County, MI... 29, 89
OCIA......... *See* Organic Crop
    Improvement Association
Offield Family Foundation
   193
OFPA.......*See* Organic Foods
    Production Act
OGM ... *See* Organic Growers
    of Michigan
Open Source Seed
    Initiative 170
Organic Advisory
    Committee............. 82, 100
Organic Certification....... *See*
    Certification
Organic Consumers
    Association 55
Organic Crop Improvement
    Association 28, 30, 53,
    98, 158
Organic Farmers of
    Michigan 28, 93, 158
Organic Farming Research
    Foundation.............. 61, 75
Organic Food Co-ops 126
Organic Foods Production
    Act 14, 34, 52, 73, 100,
    101, 133, 160, 188
*Organic Gardening and
    Farming Magazine* ...... *See*
    Rodale Press
Organic Growers Forum ...53
Organic Growers of
    Michigan 7, 16, 34, 37,
    38, 51, 52, 53, 63, 83, 84,
    94, 100, 188, 189
    Berrien chapter..............12
    By-laws.......... 8, 10, 13, 38

Central chapter....... 11, 12
    Executive Director. 12, 13,
        38
    Funding 13
    Grand Valley chapter .. 10,
        11, 12
    Lifeline chapter. 12, 16, 30
    Mid Muskegon Valley
        chapter...................... 12
    Mid-Michigan chapter.. 12
    Northwest chapter.. 12, 16
    Raisin Valley chapter ... 12
    Southeast chapter.. 11, 12,
        16, 23
    Southwest chapter. 11, 12,
        16
    State Council.... 10, 11, 12,
        13
    Third Coast chapter..... 10,
        12, 16, 21, 42
    Thornapple chapter 12
    Thumb Area chapter ... 12,
        16, 26
    Western Upper Peninsula
        chapter...................... 12
Organic Intensives...... 66, 67
Organic Soil Management
    142
Organic Tofu Cooperative 53
Organic Valley 49
Oryana Community Co-op
    .... 126, 128, 131, 133, 136,
    194
Osborne, Carol 53, 55, 61,
    64, 66, 76, 104, 190, 193,
    194
Our Stolen Future............. 67
Owasso, MI.................. 31, 93

Paul, Eldor 73
Peacewood 8
Peacework Organic Farm. 56
Pedersen-Benn, Judith..... 40
People's Food Co-op of
    Ann Arbor.... 129, 132, 194

People's Food Co-op of
Kalamazoo .. 111, 132, 194
Permaculture 108
Perry, MI 30
Perry, Ron 75
Peshkin, Rick 17
Peterson, Rich and Sheryl....22
Petoskey, MI 132, 135
Pfeiffer, Ehrenfried 187
Phillips, Ben 78
Phillips, Michael........56, 107
Phillips, Thom 106, 115
pickyourown.org 139
Pierce, Corie.......................87
Piper, Odessa.....................49
Poinsett, David 130, 131
Posselt, Gita.....................190
Predator Friendly.............169
Prelesnik, Len....................12
Prelesnik, Len and Ann 22
Priority One 174
Private Power, Public Law:
The Globalization of
Intellectual Property
Rights 165
Probyn, Laura.....................75
Purdum, Gene....................31
Purdy, Lee.....................12, 31
Purdy, Lee and Linda 30, 33
Purdy, Linda 31

Raven, Matt 89
Reams, Carey....................158
Reardon, Emily.....61, 76, 85,
86, 104, 191, 195
Reclaiming the Commons .84
Redmond, Joe.....................86
Reid, Taylor 10, 15, 115,
137, 141, 191
Renier, Sharon............42, 190
Reusch, Fred.................21, 23
Reusch, Fred and Mary.....22
Rhodes, Lynn 86
Robyn Van En Center 124
Rochdale Cooperative......126

Rockford, MI 21
Rodale Institute .. 56, 72, 175
Rodale Press ... 16, 98, 128, 188
Organic Gardening and
Farming Magazine 3,
16, 71, 187
Rodale, J.I. 3, 5, 187
Rodale, Robert 5
Rodriquez, Michael.......... 86
Roggenbuck, Les 29, 191
Rogowski, Cheryl.............. 56
Roseland Organic Farms.. 72
Rosenbaum, Robin.......... 104
Rossman, Dan 75, 100,
191, 194
Rozeboom, Dale................ 77
Ruesink, Bev 86
Rural Advancement
Foundation
International................ 63
Rutkowski, Suzanne....... 191
Ryan, Jan 190

Sacks, Adam D................ 176
Saginaw, MI 93
Samyn, Rick 191
Sanchez, Jose 75
Sandusky, MI.................... 27
SARE 45, 73, 74, 117, 192,
193
Savory, Allen................... 175
Schilder, Annemeik 75
Schmeiser, Percy 55
School of Homesteading .. 17,
18, 106, 111, 183
Schriefer, Donald L. 157
Schwallier, Phil................. 75
Score, Mike....................... 75
Scott, Paul....................... 190
Scotts, MI 42
Scrimger Farm............. 27, 28
Scrimger, Joe 26, 32, 72,
73, 83, 142, 194
Scrimger, Joe and Kay 30,
158

Scrimger, Kay 142
Sell, Susan K 165
Seminis............................165
Shettler, Emily 191
Shiawassee County, MI 31
Shultz, Bruce 10
Shultz, Paul 105
Siemon, George..................49
Silent Spring..... 71, 127, 188
Silva, George......................78
Simmons, Joe.....................75
Simmons, John 29
Skow, Dan 158
Slater, Tom 129
Sligh, Michael 56, 161
Sloan, Andrew and Nancy ...31
Smalley, Susan 42, 75, 84,
   194
Smith, J. Russell 176
Smith, Jeffrey 57
Smith, Jessie..... 78, 159, 171
Smith, Leah 78, 159, 171
Smucker, Suzanne.... 43, 191
Snapp, Sieglinde......... 78, 87
Snover, MI.................. 28, 29
Soil Biology Primer 158
Steiner, Rudolph..............186
Stevenson, Pooh.................31
Stille, Leon.......................194
Stout, Ruth 188
Student Organic Farm .... *See*
   Michigan State
   University:Student
   Organic Farm
Studier, Julia 191
Suchy, Eugene 105
Sun Dances Garden...........31
Sundin, George 75
Sunflower Farm 115
Sunshowers......................105
*Survey of Michigan Organic
   Agriculture* 76
Sustainable Agriculture
   Research and Education
   Program ....*See* SARE

Swiss Organic Agriculture
   Research Institute 54

Taylor, Ken 49
Terrill, Dane.................... 191
*The Carbon Farming
   Solution* 176
The Grain Train............. 135
The Living Soil 187
*The Many Faces of
   Community Supported
   Agriculture* 45, 117
The Organic Directory.... 3, 6
Thelen, Kurt..................... 75
Thomas, Brian 195
Thomas, Harley and Linda..31
Thompson, Collin........ 78, 89
Thorp, Lauri.................... 77
Thorton, Gary 75
Thumb of Michigan ... 26, 53,
   99
Tiedeck, Joe..................... 128
Tillers International..... 42, 111
Timeline of the Organic
   Movement.................... 186
Toensmeier, Eric............. 176
Torony, Linda.................. 191
Towne, Jon 106, 107, 108,
   109, 111
Traverse City, MI .. 125, 128,
   130
Travioli, Patti.................... 31
Tree Crops. 176
Tremble, Kay 66
Treter, Chris 55
Tri-County Organic Farm
   and Garden Club 4
Tumalla, Lal..................... 71
Turtle Island Farm 21, 22

USDA........ 34, 51, 52, 58, 68,
   74, 82, 87, 89, 133, 134,
   143, 160, 169, 189
   Natural Resources
   Conservation Service ...87

USDA
  Risk Management
    Agency 87, 88

Valenti, John 39, 190
Van Wormer, Heather.....118
VanVoorhees, John..........191
Vondrasek, Bill 31

Wall, Barney & Delores ..190
Walters, Chris..................159
Ware, Bernie and Sandee ..194
Ware Farm 44
Warner, Karen..................191
Warnke, John and Patti..195
Washtenaw Community
    College............................41
Waters, Charles...............157
Wayne State University..112
Weilnau, Al 20
Wesala, Lisa...............42, 190
Western Michigan
    University 1, 105, 106,
    107, 108, 183
Westwind Farm 31, 33
Westwind Milling 53
Whalon, Mark....................75
Whealy, Kent 49
Wheeler, Phil 32

Whetham Organic Farm .. 37
Whetham, Pat....4, 14, 19, 31,
    34, 37, 39, 40, 41, 42, 43, 44,
    52, 64, 83, 103, 190, 195
Who Owns Organic? 161
Whole Foods 192
Williamsburg, MI 3
Wilson College 124
Wisconsin Historical
    Society 1
Wissman, Ilda 8
Withey, Patty 195
WMU *See* Western Michigan
    University
World War II 187
Wyant, Dan 103

Yaeger, John 7, 8, 11
Yaeger, John and Judy.....7, 16
Yaeger, Judy 7, 8, 15
Yeomans, Allan............... 174
Ypsilanti Food Co-op 132
Ypsilanti, MI 41, 132

Zabadal, Tom 75
Zennie, Tom 55
Zennie, Tom and Nancy ... 22
Zimba, Ed 100
Zimmerman, Maggie 129

Made in the USA
San Bernardino, CA
25 June 2017